What Others Are Saying.

"*Career Ownership: Creating 'Job Security' in Any Economy* is a roadmap for change for both employees and employers. Both win when there is a shared responsibility and ownership of the worker's career asset."

Michael Haubrich, CFP, Financial Service Group, Inc. & Creator of the Career Asset Management Model

"Janine powerfully combines her years of experience as a leader and a coach with metaphor, and thoughtful analysis of what really needs to change for today's businesses and their workers to succeed."

Marcia Bench, Serial Entrepreneur, Author, and Purposeful Business Strategist & Founder, Career Coach Institute

"*Career Ownership* is a story that needs to be told. We have the opportunity to create our own futures...invest in our own careers...shape our own destinies. Career Ownership will be our roadmap. Let's get started. Henry Ford has left the building...."

Ken Lazar, Founder Scioto Ridge Job Networking Group, LLC

"It's a perfect guide for a new era, mixing warm rich storytelling with practical guides for discovering your path to work that makes a difference, to control of your career and toward a more authentic life."

Ray Taylor, Region Manager Standard Register Healthcare Business Unit

"*Career Ownership* is a tremendous advantage for business owners who want to retain talented employees. At H.R. Gray, we recognize that the commitment of our upcoming leaders is what that drives our success over the long term. We now have that advantage after successfully implementing this program with 20 of our associates."

James P. Joyce, P. E., President and CEO H.R. Gray

CAREER OWNERSHIP
CREATING 'JOB SECURITY' IN ANY ECONOMY

JANINE MOON

Career Ownership
Creating 'Job Security' in Any Economy

Published by:

Parker & Shelby Press, a division of CompassPoint Coaching LLC
Columbus, Ohio

Editor: Bonnie Budzowski, Incredible Messages
Cover art and design: James Hazelett, Immortal Nights
Cover photography: Rick Yocum, Lara Moon

First edition
ISBN: 978-0-615-35337-1

Library of Congress Control Number: 2010925356

Printed in the United States of America

How to order:
Copies may be ordered from CompassPoint Coaching.
Quantity discount available by calling 614.488-6876,
or visit http://workforcechange.com/careerownership .

To my daughter, Lara

who encourages me
to be a better person
than I am

Acknowledgments

A lifelong fascination with work and career and using the talents I've been given is the catalyst for this book. And it's the people who have been part of my work life that I want to thank: those who challenged me and taught me; who in doing so provided the energy to define what I knew was missing and write it down.

Many will be unnamed because they are part of my 20-year love-hate relationship with corporate America. It's too far in my past to remember all the names, and for the most part, they were people from whom I learned how not to do things. My guess is you know who you are: thank you.

Over the last nine years, I've had the privilege of coaching hundreds of clients who were looking for something more, who wanted to make a difference through their own talents. Thanks to each individual for trusting me to be a guide, and for providing the opportunity to solidify my beliefs about work and careers in the 21st century.

A special notice for good friends and colleagues who encouraged me along this journey: Rick, Laurie, Cinzia, Tami, my Mastermind partners and other "tweeps" who sent words of support.

Truly special thanks to Michael Haubrich for believing in this work when few others did. It's been so important that he gets it.

Thanks to Rick and Nancy for willingly reading portions of the manuscript and providing valuable comments and observations.

The Glorious Gator Gals, Mary & Gloria, have been my consistent Buds for a lot of years; they listened to me talk over miles of trails and roads, especially as we trained for the Disney Marathon. Mary is my Rhoda: she ran the marathon because I wanted to do it. Now, that's an incredible friend.

And my love to Lara, my beautiful chip off the old block who's designing her life intentionally, wisely and with spirit. She's my muse…more than she'll ever know.

Preface

> "It's not supposed to be fun...
> that's why it's called work!"
>
> - Edith David Mossing (1919-1997)

I doubt my mother, Edith Mossing, ever thought she would be quoted in a book, and I certainly never expected that the book would be mine. But with a strange sort of karma, her words may have been the spark for my fascination with, well, work.

Having grown up on a farm, I know what work is: it's toil, manual labor, sweat, drudgery, etc., etc. I also know the difference between work (paid) and work (unpaid). I learned the latter from about the age of seven, wielding a hoe up and down rows of corn and soybeans on my family's farm in northwest Ohio. And from age seven until the age of 16, when I walked into Holly's Restaurant and started as a waitress, I dreamed about how much better paid work would be.

Considering the two types of work above, I still think paid is better. But I've also expanded my thoughts about work to encompass much more. Besides waitressing, I've worked in box and wire factories, as a high school English, Speech and drama teacher, a bowling and golf coach, a curriculum developer, manager, lobbyist and executive. I found each type of work fascinating, challenging and learning-filled. For a variety of reasons, I never stayed in one place long enough to get bored… and I always left with a little more savoir-faire than I had when I started.

It might have been this relatively consistent turnover in my work that made me focus on the path, or really the lack of a planned path, of my career. I went from one position to another, creating the work as I went most of the time, leveraging my strengths to accomplish the tasks and to take satisfaction in doing so. As I did, the industries I worked in and the world itself were changing. The organizations I was part of downsized or grew as the business required, and I aligned myself, my projects and my associates to keep pace and sometimes lead the changes.

So I didn't have a defined career path, but I certainly had a career direction: it was always the next challenge or initiative that moved the bigger picture forward. Somehow I sized it up and morphed into the worker with the skills and abilities needed to accomplish the job. In that, I was different from my peers. I never knew what my next "job title" would be or how long I should stay in one position. My path defied the traditional paths inside organizations, and truth be told, I liked it that way.

Even as a single mom, I never hung my hat on "cradle-to-grave" or "40-and-out." I thought staying with the same organization—especially when its leaders chose to do things as they'd always been done—was a real waste of abilities. I saw people all around me who had retired at their desks, yet were always awake to collect a Friday paycheck. I saw bright, talented people leave because they hadn't paid enough dues to advance or because their position in the hierarchy labeled them as "peon" rather than "leader." Moving to another organization usually resulted in a repeat experience or worse. I also knew bright, talented people who stayed and lost their belief in themselves to the arrogance and disdain of people at the top.

So it's this combination of experience and learning that gives me the wisdom to say "Career Ownership is the only security you have." Because I made a lot of change, led a lot of change and lived with the resistance, I saw first-hand the misery inherent in the clash of Industrial economy management and leadership with knowledge workers. I left my last corporate position before all of the life was sucked out of me and before I gave in to an organization culture that cherished only physical assets, never human ones. I could see so clearly the need for brains and heart and soul; yet each morning I tripped over the "emotions bucket" just outside the employee entrance…and it was always full.

When I looked around to find advances in career thinking and development, I came up short. Most organizations were too busy using Industrial age solutions to deal with global competitors to give much thought to employee careers. Employees, socialized to wait for direction from above, continued to wait, wasting both their time and talent as the economy transformed "jobs" into "project work."

Seeing my own frustrations reflected in others led me to career coaching and coach-specific training to guide people in finding their best work direction. I eventually achieved certification as one of five Master Certified Career Coaches in the United States.

Over the last nine years I've met with central Ohio job seekers on a monthly basis at local Execunet meetings. As an executive and career coach, I've worked with many hundreds of individuals from around the world who want satisfaction in how they spend their working hours. They want to contribute to a bigger goal than the weekly report for the regional manager. They want to know they matter. I see people who have lost their spirit and whose emotional health is destroyed in their work environments. I see people who are lost in today's employment market and whose defense mechanism is pulling their blinders tighter.

All this to say that I've experienced and guided enough change and I've collected enough work- wisdom to know that there has to be a better way: for people to make a living and know they make a difference, for businesses to be successful in a tremendously competitive economy and for some balance between an organization's need for human capital and its desire for human control.

I call that better way Career Ownership.

It's a different approach to getting work done and getting the right workers in the right seats. Career Ownership shifts the responsibility from the organization to the worker for providing value, for being flexible and resilient and for adjusting to changing business strategy. It places the responsibility on the organization for treating its human capital as valuable assets and for recognizing that "all brains on deck" is a requirement in a competitive world.

It makes the organization responsible for leveraging intrinsic motivation and for only hiring and promoting managers who have proven skills in building collaborative relationships and in developing associates' talents.

I wrote this book to help you solve a problem that's not going away, and to live in an economy that's never going back to "how it used to be." "Job security" as defined in the informal employment contract of the 20th century is gone. But job security can still exist—you just need to make it happen. This book is a guide to doing so. In fact, it's a guide to more than the security people desire; it's a guide to the work and career satisfaction they want, too.

This book is for you whether you want to stay in your organization or leave. Many of my coaching clients who are intent on going to another organization change their minds when they learn more about their organization, explore it for possible work matches, clarify their own value to the business and seek the wisdom and support of mentors. They discover opportunities when they reframe their definition of work.

So, that's how I see work working; that's why I wrote this book. Work doesn't have to be "hard" in the same way it was on the farm or in the factory; and whether paid or unpaid, humans still desire to make a difference, to give something back to the world, and to do work that touches them emotionally and spiritually. In the 21st century, America's businesses and society need that, too.

> Note: Throughout the book I consciously use the word "work" rather than job. "Job" signifies some level of responsibility that you step into and out of during certain hours under certain conditions. "Work" is something you do because it's your contribution, it's an expression of your talents, and it's your heart and soul. Your work is distinctly you and the contribution only you can make to your organization's mission.

Contents

> You have brains in your head.
> You have feet in your shoes.
> You can steer yourself
> any direction you choose.
>
> - Dr. Seuss, American Author,
> *Oh the Places You'll Go!*

Chapter 1: Do You Know Your Way to Work?

Over the last few years Americans have discovered new levels of unemployment and frustration resulting from changed employment markets. Some experts say "the next few years will be rough and then jobs will come back strong." Others say "we'll never have that late 20th century heyday again." I'm in the latter camp. Overwhelming evidence suggests the changes in the job market are permanent. The sooner we accept this, the sooner we can build the skills we need to become valuable in the workplace and build the job security we desire.

Not only has the manufacturing base turned from manual to robotic, the paperless office (while never quite literal) has become portable and efficient, requiring fewer paper pushers. The U.S. workforce has increased productivity over the last several decades due to technology and intentional focus on "lean and mean" labor forces. While productivity is good, it means fewer workers.

The workforce has seen organizations changing the core of their businesses in an effort to compete in a global marketplace with different rules and diverse customers. Some of the changes have included sending work to less costly labor forces outside of the U.S. in order to remain competitive. Others have included hiring more contractors or temporary workers to better align with fluctuating markets.

All the while, those affected by the tremendous workforce changes are all too easily swayed—by fear, denial and *the comfort of the known*—into putting on blinders and thinking, "the next job will last."

Business and economic reality tells us otherwise.

Oh, there is still plenty of work to do. Businesses need the brains and hearts of employees more than ever: these are the source of innovation and service and the human connection that ensures return customers. But depending upon the industry, the market and the competitors, the work doesn't fit as easily as it used to into "job boxes" of 40 hours a week. How work gets done is changing and hiring practices reflect that. But Americans looking for work and those looking for a better job "when the economy improves" are still longing for the good old days. They choose not to recognize that career paths, ladders and "job security" are anachronistic memories from a different economy.

Work today requires flexible, innovative, resilient *dancers:* those who can upgrade their skills and turn on a dime to respond to customer and market needs. No job description can prescribe how to do this, and so fewer "jobs" and more "contracts" is a smart business response. It's time for employees to catch up and become those valuable assets that U.S. organizations need.

Career Ownership provides the map that "employees" need in order to be recognized as "assets" and to partner with employers. It puts the responsibility for being in the right place at the right time doing the right work on the worker, who as an individual can "dance" so much more flexibly than can any business. Career Ownership is a model that is 180 degrees from a traditional career approach, but it's one that mirrors the needs of people and business. It's based on self-knowledge and awareness of business direction and shows how the alignment of the two can create the value needed by today's organizations and the security desired by workers.

Career ownership is the path to career security

Career Ownership enables you to take control of your work results and career direction. Just as the move from renting to owning your home becomes the first big investment milestone for many people—the first step toward control of lifelong assets—the move to career ownership is a first milestone toward building equity in your work security. In both cases, ownership provides stability, deep satisfaction, and a long-term planning opportunity for the future.

This book helps you take these first steps in an orderly way. You begin by gaining clarity on what's really important and where your value truly lies in any work setting. The worksheets included (and available on the web in full size) make sure you do the investigation and analysis in a logical progression and get support for completing the journey to ownership.

Career Ownership is a process that allows you to take responsibility for your own career direction—in any organization—at any time. It prepares you to:

- Define the learning and experience you need to be successful, based upon your talents and desires…
  your uniqueness

- Determine your value as an asset to any organization

- Define possible career paths in any organization

- Build a business case for squaring up your career direction and development needs with your organization's strategy and goals.

No more waiting to see if someone in the organization thinks you're worth developing or recognizes your value. You can define yourself as an asset, provide the results that your target organization desires and choose to realign yourself in the same company or one that offers a better fit.

It's your career. It's time to own it.

How to use this book

Just read it—to pique your thinking and to take action toward providing more value to your "career customer" while creating more security in return. Considering every organization as your "customer" is perhaps the first shift in your thinking but one you will use throughout your work life. Every customer may not need the services you provide, but the Career Ownership model helps you identify and create value for those that do.

Begin by reading the first four chapters so you have a clear picture of today's employment and work environments. Chapter Four, in particular, asks you to take a focused look at your world view to see if you're sabotaging yourself. Chapters five through ten give you a map for career ownership: you start by clarifying your Foundation because knowing yourself is at the core of ownership. That's followed by learning about your customer, determining mentors and opportunities and finally, making the business case for your career direction. Using the worksheets at the end of those chapters allows you to learn as you go, and to reflect a little at a time.

Career Ownership is a guide for landscape that has and continues to change, so feel free to use the sections that are useful to you and within your own timeframes. Your own situation, experiences and attention to opportunities—viewed through eyes wide open—are the best guides to a career direction that works for you.

> *No one can build his security*
> *upon the nobleness of another person.*
>
> - Willa Cather, American Author

Chapter 2: When Was the Last Time You Washed a Rental Car?

Look at *Table 1* below and check the boxes as they apply to you:

Item	Do you own it or rent it?	Whether 'rent' or 'own,' why?
House		
Auto		
Furniture		

Table 1: *Options for Renting and Owning*

The American Way, among other things, is about ownership. Chances are you own your home, your car, and your furniture. Ownership represents stability, security, safety, and success. For many, financial portfolios are built around their homes. The very last thing to go in hard times is a home: it's a haven, a rock that provides security that little else can. While owning their own home might be a given to my readers, owning their work is not necessarily so.

In American society, owning your own home is also a grown-up thing to do: buying your first house is a major milestone. In our society, it signals the move from fun and youth to responsible, mature adult. When you take on home ownership, you become master of your own fate, accepting the responsibility that comes with it and stepping into your place as a citizen of your community and the world. You become the decision maker, the one who makes and implements strategic plans for your home. You make plans and take action to ensure two things. First, you take action to maximize your enjoyment of this place—the one where you spend a significant portion of your time. Second, you take action to maintain and increase the value of your investment.

Here are things homeowners typically do when planning and living in their homes. It's likely these are actions are familiar to you:

- Conscientiously save until they can afford the home that will really make them happy

- Choose a stable location where their investment has a high probability of increasing its value

- Choose a home and location that gives them pleasure— promising to be appealing to them and their loved ones over the long term

- Research and purchase insurance against disasters they cannot control

- Devote time and funds to routine upkeep and maintenance

- Repair problems before they get out of hand

- Invest in visual appeal—curb appeal for real estate value, and internal appeal for personal pleasure

- Educate themselves with books, online resources, home shows, TV shows

- Actively build positive relationships with neighbors and others who impact the value of the home experience

- Hire a professional when needed

- Make strategic plans for improvements to enhance quality of life and financial returns

- Save in anticipation of implementing plans

Home ownership is time-consuming, expensive and often inconvenient. Who wants to shovel snow, clean gutters and pay for roof repairs? For most of us, it's difficult to even unravel our own motivation for home ownership. We own our homes, in large part, because we want to control our own destiny, arrange our space to please ourselves, and control our own financial futures. And everyone around us expects us to be homeowners once we reach a certain maturity level. So we rise to the occasion and never look back.

Why, then, do so many of us own our homes but rent our careers? Why is it that the one thing that is the source of security—our work, our career, our livelihood—is the one thing that we give up to someone else, without even making a fuss? Before you protest too loudly with "I don't want to be an entrepreneur," or "Of course I own my career; nobody else pays any attention to it," consider these questions:

- When did you last consider your career "location?" Does it provide maximum satisfaction and the promise of enduring value for the investment you've made in your work life?

- When did you last do serious research to educate yourself about the future of your industry and the skills needed to succeed in this changing marketplace?

- When did you last assess your skills, abilities, and goals to determine how you could get the most satisfaction out of the workspace in which you spend many of your waking hours?

- When did you last write out (of your own volition) your 3-year career plan along with your 12-month learning plan…and follow them?

- When did you last devote personal time and funds to upgrade your own skills?

- When did you last consider requesting a job rotation that would help you build relationships and impact your marketability inside or outside of your organization?

- When did you last talk to your manager about the additional value you provide to your clients and how you accomplish this?

- When did you last review and align yourself with your organization's top two strategic growth areas?

- When did you last identify a weak area in your skills or performance and take personal responsibility to address the problem?

- When did you last have a conversation about how your work life circumstances impact the important others in your life?

Yes, these steps are time-consuming, expensive and often inconvenient. Until you've done these things, however, you don't own your career. You do not control your own livelihood. You are assuming that someone else will do this… it's the default position. But in today's world, if *you* aren't managing your career, then you are leaving it up to chance.

Attributed to several people, this statement *is* the definitive spin on owning (anything) v. renting (anything): "Nobody ever washes a rental car." Now, think about that. Chances are you have rented a car before. When was the last time you washed that car before you returned it? And, if the truth be known, would you fill the car with gas before returning it if the penalty for *not* doing so wasn't outrageous?

The truth is that we take better care of things we own. We wash the cars we own and change the oil on schedule. We keep our homes maintained, recognizing that the house is more than a shelter; it's an investment in our own future. We pay attention to the local school system, to the tax base, to the community in which we reside to ensure that our investment continues to grow. We value this freedom and self-reliance, taking pride of ownership.

Somehow, pride of ownership in our work has never quite taken root in the United States. Most of us joined organizations and expected our managers and the Human Resources folks to guide us along the steps to a successful career. Baby boomers, especially, grew up with an expectation of cradle-to-grave job security. They believed that if they worked hard, were loyal to the company and paid their dues, they'd be rewarded with promotions and job security. Even now, when the doctrine of "cradle-to-grave" clearly no longer exists, most workers are still passive about their careers.

Oddly, even today's youngest workers--those of Generation X and the Millennial generation—while growing up with different work values, are not prepared to take responsibility for their own careers. Perhaps this is because there are few role models or mentors to point the way to career ownership. This represents a crisis in our culture because the rent-a-job view doesn't work anymore—for organizations or for workers.

Do you recognize yourself in these scenarios?

Terry, 22, has stopped going to college because he wants to do work that matters. He doesn't know what that is, but he knows that taking classes without a direction is more frustrating than fun. He can't figure out how to mesh his love of video gaming with work that makes enough money for a comfortable life, but he knows that his work has to make a difference.

Tim, late 30's, loves the work of his profession and he's really good at it…but he's been promoted to management so doesn't get to do much technical work. Actually the only time he gets to do the work is when he's frustrated with his employees and takes over the work to do it right. He knows that this hurts his employees as well as his effectiveness as a manager. He wants to be a good leader but right now Tom has limited challenge and no clear career direction. While he's tried to talk with his boss about his direction, his boss believes money fixes everything and that "work is work."

Joe, early 30s, likes his profession and the organization he works for. It has a great 'family' feeling, and that's important, but nobody ever talks to him about his future. He wants to move up, he thinks, although he doesn't want 60-hour weeks like his dad. He doesn't really see many steps in the organization, and since no one is talking to him about it, maybe that means he doesn't have a future here and he'd better keep his eyes open.

Anne, early 50s, has moved around in her work. While trained in broadcasting, she's done event planning, sales and has landed in retail. Now with no sense of direction, and yet a strong desire to make a difference Anne wants to figure it out. She's tired of being bored and frustrated while knowing she could contribute to something bigger.

The people in each of these scenarios have something in common with each other and likely with you. Each individual is longing for satisfying, more meaningful work and yet has given up career direction to someone else. Each is relying on a manager who *might* discuss his or her career path during the annual performance review. Perhaps each is also waiting for the Human Resources/Training department to provide training for next career steps.

The unstated but underlying belief in each scenario is that somebody else will define what comes next. If that doesn't happen, and the individual becomes increasingly unhappy, leaving is an option—but no one ever does before it's absolutely necessary. If people don't own their career future, they are—by default—waiting until someone else steps in to do it for them. For most everyone, that's a long wait.

And in the economy of the 21st century, people who decide to leave their jobs will find fewer options. Four generations now compete for the same positions; businesses change strategies more often than a couch potato changes channels; cut-backs and technological efficiencies have created lean workforces; and few organizations put any focus on career paths or development. While jobs may be tougher to land, the work hasn't gone away. It's changed, packaged differently, and may require new skills but the need for people to provide service and develop new customer offerings is still there. It's what the economy runs on!

Workers caught in down-sizings, right-sizings, or layoffs walk around in a daze because the employment market has changed—and they aren't prepared. They go to job clubs, try valiantly to network even though they hate it and wonder if it works. They send resumes with abandon, and secretly ask: "Why me?" The tape inside their heads says: "I've worked hard all my life, I followed the rules, I did whatever my boss told me to do, I played politics, I was a good soldier. It's not fair."

And, they are right—it's not fair. It will never be "fair" because **it's a different game**. Just like the rules are different for Wii and Monopoly, so too are the rules different for today's work. You only win at Wii when you get up from the table and board, grab the controller and put your whole self into the electronic game at hand. It's the same with today's workplaces and employment market: you only 'win' when you shift your mindset to the rules of today's economy and strategize within those rules.

The Only Rule:
Your career belongs to you.
It's your responsibility. You'd better own it.

The irony here is that neither we nor the organization benefits when we're passive about our careers. In today's competitive environment, organizations don't need passive, disengaged workers—stuck in their job boxes waiting to be told what to do. They need doers and thinkers who put creativity, passion, and energy into their work. Organizations prefer to pay people who make a difference by connecting with their customers because they love what they do, over those who simply put in time.

We are most engaged and satisfied when we bring our best selves to work. We do better work when we care... it's human. Organizations need us to bring our best to the workplace. So, if we both need the same thing, what's the dilemma?

Both employers and employees are stuck in a paternalistic, rent-a-job, up-is-the-only-way career model. What both sides really need is employees who take ownership of their work and see that it provides ongoing value.

Why not "blink first?" Take the initiative: stop waiting to be picked, to be directed and start doing. You're the one who can align your contributions with the organization's goals, but you have to step out of your job box to do so. Take your share of responsibility for where the business is going, and how it's attracting and retaining customers. You are in position to see small changes that can make a big difference, which leaders often cannot. If what you change contributes to the bigger goals, why wouldn't you do it? Assess the risk, toss out your unfounded fear and do whatever keeps your customers coming back. You are creating security.

On your job description write:
No boundaries. Do whatever needs to be done.
Ask forgiveness, not permission.

Take aways:

1. This economy requires more of you and different parts of you than you've been expected to provide in the past. The game is new and you must learn to play by the new rules.

2. What makes you human is what you can contribute most to this new game: your talents, initiative, and authentic self—your heart and soul.

3. It's up to you to step up, step in and matter.

> *It is not the strongest of the species that survives, nor the most intelligent that survives. It is the one that is the most adaptable to change.*
>
> - Charles Darwin
> Scientist, Theory of Evolution

Chapter 3: Do you feel the earth move under your feet?

Imagine this: you get up at dawn, throw on some old clothes, grab breakfast and your cold thermos, and head out the door, picking up a hoe as you pass the shed. You check the blade and, finding it dull, you wander into the shed for a file to sharpen the edge. You do this as slowly as you can possibly get away with, knowing the day will be both long and hot. With the sun just breaking the horizon, you head out to the soybean fields to get a head-start on the day's heat. You'll spend the day in 90-degree weather walking the rows of soybeans, hoeing out thistles, milk weeds, and stray corn stalks. The cleaner the beans come harvest time, the better the crop.

Hoeing bean fields on the family farm was my first job. During the 1960's most of the country worked in businesses and factories—the industrial economy. My family lived in an agrarian one. We were certainly in the minority, but family farms were prevalent in northwest Ohio, and ours had been in the family for generations. I hated hoeing soybeans, but I did it until I was 16.

I knew about the industrial economy; they paid you directly. My Dad supplemented the farm income in bad years by working during the winters at the Willis Jeep factory in Toledo. I don't really know what my dad did, but I do remember that it was important for him to arrive on time, to work until the end of his shift and to do the job he was hired to do. In return, my Dad collected a paycheck every two weeks.

I was part of the "seam," or the transition from farming to non-farm business—I had a foot in both camps. While family farms still exist, farming has changed considerably to account for technology improvements and the economic realities of the world. Farms are bigger and must employ the economies of scale and advanced technologies to survive.

Look at the circles in **Figure 1.** They represent a proportional view of today's existing economies. The agrarian economy gave way to the industrial economy. The industrial economy has given way to the information / service economy. And within that economy is one focused on innovation and creativity, the conceptual economy. All of these economies still exist, of course, in various stages of growth or decline.

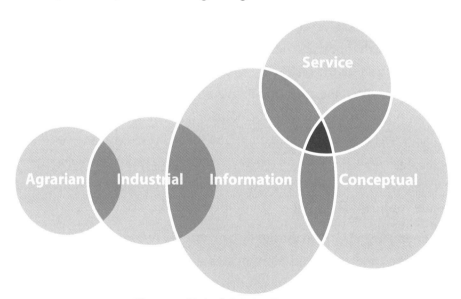

Figure 1: *Today's Existing Economies*

Just as I grew up during a seam, in the shift from the agrarian economy to the industrial one, we are now in the midst of another seam. Farms are still around, but in much smaller numbers. The industrial machine is shrinking before our eyes. The reality of today's economic landscape, however, is this: most work that is valued and paid for at a premium involves brains and not much brawn. Global business has changed the landscape of not only *what* work is valued, but *how valuable* it is.

Undeveloped and underdeveloped countries have become educated enough that their labor forces can replicate the work of the U.S. workforce and for a great deal less money. With a strategy of controlling expenses, many businesses see lower labor costs as low-hanging fruit. What has traditionally been the backbone of our American economy—factories and white collar paperwork—is no more, because that work has been made efficient by technology and less costly through outsourced labor.

Table 2 highlights differences among today's economies.

Element	Agrarian	Industrial	Info / Service and Conceptual
Labor	Hard physical labor; season-driven; limited education needed	Some physical labor; fit the assigned mold; education needed to move up	Limited physical; principally mental; few standard operating procedures
Rewards	Livelihood; self-reliance	40-hours work for 40-hours pay every 2 weeks; career paths; cradle-to-grave employment	Innovation, right-brain valued; self-reliance; variety; constant learning
Drawbacks	Weather-dependent and local market dependent	Dependent upon executive decisions; initiative not important	Global economy = global competition; initiative critical; left-brain work easily outsourced

Table 2: *How today's economies compare*

So you're in that seam: the workscape has changed and you have a choice. You can hope to hang onto one of the diminishing white collar jobs in the industrial employment market, or you can figure out how to step into the new economy and get paid what you're worth. In the seam or transition between the agrarian and industrial economies, the answer was college education and conformity. Along with a good "yes man" attitude, a college degree became the ticket to get you into the coveted white collar ranks and move you up the ladder of leadership. In today's seam and organizations, it takes a lot more. Businesses need employees who know their value and align, collaborate, capitalize on their strengths, get the best from others and create results that fulfill the organization's mission.

The answer for today's seam is still education, but in a different capacity. Education in today's economy never stops, and what's important is that you can manipulate your knowledge and learning and experience into different results: intriguing, distinctive and connection-creating ideas and outcomes. It's still an economy about products and services for customers, but the results must be anything but cookie cutter. Who would have thought, for example, that an iPhone meditation app and one for dictionary.com would be among the most popular? Someone did: by connecting iPhones, users, problems and how to build a better wheel, there are now multitudes of delighted iPhone owners who experience 'om' whenever they like and spell it correctly, too!

So, it's up to you: you can hold on as long as you're able, doing the work you're told to do, putting in the hours you're told to put in, hoping that "they" don't lay you off. Or you can move to the real world where strategically managing your contributions of brains, initiative and creativity create your security.

I know, I know: you're comfortable where you are. You like going to work and picking up a paycheck every couple of weeks. You know your job inside and out and don't have to think too hard. You're in a rut but this all seems like a lot of work to do something you might not be very good at or might not be able to learn, at least not without a lot of effort. This is your emotional brain talking, the voice inside your head that loves to stay comfortable and safe. You can make the change if you want to, but you have to intentionally choose it and get beyond the voice.

Moving from renting to owning is scary…but very, very smart

The change is very much like renting v. owning. Owning your home is often time-consuming and inconvenient. It involves more risks than renting, and a different mind set. As a renter, you use someone else's stuff and often treat it as expendable. With your own stuff, you handle it differently, maintain or preserve it regularly, and are choosy about who you let borrow it. When we own something, we have greater responsibility and more recognition of the long-term investment. Career Ownership is just that different. It takes different skills, different preparation, different equipment and, maybe most important of all, a higher level of responsibility and personal investment. So why would you ever choose to leave the comfort of the way things are?

Because renting is no longer a viable option. As the economy changes, renting conveys a message of passivity and lack of engagement to your employer and potential employers. It says you're expecting to work under the old rules, that you value your comfort over the organization's success and you want no share in the responsibility of a shifting economy. When you send this message, you become dead weight. You indicate that your flexibility is limited and your comfort comes first, and you like to do things your way…the old way. When circumstances set you up to be compared with employees who actively bring all of themselves (brain, heart, soul) to work, your job will be at real risk.

The changing paradigm about what constitutes a desirable employee may have crept up on you. Plenty of good, responsible individuals—like Jerry in the Case Study described in Figure 2— have been caught unaware. People who gave 10, 15, or even 30 years of solid service are now struggling to catch up with the new job market as downsizing and other changes have caught up with them.

Where's the value—experience v. relevance?

Jerry had been searching for his next position in the supply chain function for almost three years. He talked about 'coming close' but being frustrated by what potential employers were asking of him. Several wanted Jerry to do contract work. But what Jerry really wanted was a 'guarantee' that in exchange for his 30-year accumulation of knowledge, he would have a certain length of employment. He expected that his experience defined his value.

What Jerry neglected to consider is that the organization could—over a very short period of time—find its employees' skills outdated and irrelevant to the market. Saddled with experienced but irrelevant workers, the company's ability to respond to its customers could be seriously harmed. Jerry's outdated employment view became the obstacle to the very security he desired.

Figure 2: *Case Study: Where's the value—experience v. relevance?*

Take aways:

1. Today's global economy requires different work.

2. We're living in a seam: that place where two items are joined. Our seam is where the industrial and informational/service economies meet.

3. Moving from the comfort of a known economy to a different one requires new abilities and mindsets.

> *It is essential to employ, trust, and reward those whose perspective, ability, and judgment are radically different from yours. It is also rare, for it requires uncommon humility, tolerance, and wisdom.*
>
> - Dee W. Hock, Fast Company,
> Founder of Visa International

Chapter 4: Mindsets and Money: Are You in Your Own Way?

Mindsets are how we see the world. Also called 'world views,' these are the filters through which we test our actions and interactions and make our way through life.

Our mindsets are formed from all of the learning, shaping and experiences we have throughout our lives. Much of our world view comes from our families, childhood experiences and school. We pick up beliefs and assumptions from early conditioning. This is natural since we "belong" to our families, classes, and teams based upon learning how other people in our lives think and act.

We have beliefs about money, work, friendships, values, right and wrong—the list is endless. Often these assumptions are valuable: they keep us safe, make us social and polite, and serve us well in business, family and the community. As we experience more, we may update our world views because we learn new things and our reality changes. Problems arise when we don't make the changes.

For example, many of you probably had a curfew when you were younger. Parents put limits in place for safety purposes and for teaching responsibility. While you lived under your parents' roof, you adhered to your curfew or chose to suffer the consequences. When you moved out on your own, however, did you still keep the curfew?

Most likely not. When you became the "responsible adult" and made your own decisions, you "updated" your world view of curfews. You questioned the assumptions about curfew and removed a restriction that no longer made sense. You opened a world of new night time possibilities!

Mindsets get in our way when we don't update our world views to keep up with reality. Sometimes a physical reality makes us change. You may not place a value on eating well and exercising regularly, but your body may tell you differently. You may become ill or lack energy for your favorite activities. Your doctor may help you decide that it's in your best interest to change your behaviors.

Are your work and money mindsets holding you back?

Some of the toughest world views to update are those around work and money. They often come out as "shoulds" and sound like this:

- I should be considered a valuable employee; I have more than 30 years experience in my field.

- I shouldn't have to worry about being downsized; I have seniority in this department.

- My manager should be telling me what (training) I need to be a better employee...that's not my job.

- I should have gotten the promotion that went to the younger guy; they must think I'm too old and that's not fair or legal.

- I should be on the 'up and comers' list because upper management knows I do good work.

- Things should get better if I just wait this out; I've only got 12 years to retirement.

- My career path should be "up;" no other direction is really considered successful.

Each statement reflects an outdated mindset. They originate from the more regimented and standardized workplaces of the 20th century. They are no longer accurate. If these beliefs are part of your mindset, you are harming yourself and your future earning capacity. It's critical that you update your world view about how work works today. Career Ownership can help you do that.

Money views also can sabotage how you see your career and who owns it. Do you have any money assumptions that sound like these?

- There's never enough.

- If I made more money, things would be better.

- I need to keep my nose to the grindstone until my kids are out of college.

- If I change my direction now, all of my experience is wasted.

- I need to make more money each year—how else can we keep up?

- I can't afford to go back to school if my employer won't pay for it.

- There is no such thing as doing work you love. It has to be hard in order to get paid for it.

- I don't think I can make a living doing something else—this is all I know.

- I'm afraid to change my career direction—I might have to take less money.

- I can't afford to slow down even if my blood pressure is high; I run the risk of being part of the next round of layoffs.

- How will we live if I lose my job?

Each of these beliefs and assumptions is based on fear and outdated thinking. If the price of hanging onto any one of them is stress, frustration, or constant fear, you need to let them go. Recognize that you can change them if you choose.

Your greatest chance for successfully shifting your mindset is to get the support of objective observers who can help you separate your emotions from facts and guide you toward logical thinking. A career coach is one, and your financial advisor is another.

Objective observers are a good idea

An experienced career coach can help you examine assumptions that may be sabotaging your career direction, especially those that are out of touch with business reality. Only you can change or shift your beliefs, but a coach can help you examine how your beliefs serve you—or not.

Certified Financial Planners are beginning to help their clients consider "career" as a financial asset, especially with the continuing demographic and employment trends that impact the economy. One CFP, Michael Haubrich of Financial Service Group, has developed a Career Asset Management Model (CAMM) that he uses with clients to guide them in examining their career plans and direction. He incorporates the CAMM model into the review of financial plans and includes career as a class of assets, like stocks, bonds, real estate and cash. One of the tools Mr. Haubrich uses is a "Career Asset Working Capital Fund," which is a reserve fund that helps a client increase the value of their career asset. The dollars in this "working capital" fund are used for skills upgrades, for funding career transitions, and even for career sabbaticals.

With this kind of planning and financial wherewithal, the possibility for taking more direct responsibility for your career becomes feasible. Think about it within the "ownership" analogy: we plan our life changing decisions so that we can be prepared and increase our chances of success.

Planning shapes outcomes

Before you bought your first home (or if you're now considering it), you likely did plenty of studying and investigation so you had greater confidence in your decision. You probably saved for a down payment, studied neighborhoods and schools, ran the numbers on your income and expenses, and even began saving for improvements and maintenance.

And even before deciding to adopt a pet, you probably considered these issues: what size animal will fit best with your lifestyle? What kinds of expenses will you have or are there likely medical costs? Who will take care of your pet if have to work late or travel? How will you provide care during vacations?

By thinking and planning ahead of time, even big decisions become realistic and reduce your risk of moving forward. Especially when you get the support of professionals who can ensure that you've thought things through thoroughly and logically, made plans and back-up plans, and developed a budget that works within your desired lifestyle, your risks decrease and your rewards are more certain.

Your emotions and outdated world views don't have to hold you back from taking ownership of your career. Tap the expertise of people who can guide and support you. Combine their expertise with the Career Ownership model and you will leverage the value of your career into one that serves you for a lifetime.

Take aways:

1. Because we can't see them and they are often emotional, our mindsets around money and work can easily sabotage us.

2. Mindsets must be updated to include the reality of 21st century work and careers and changes in the economy.

3. Keeping your world views current helps ensure that your decisions around career, money and other life issues serve you.

Talking the Talk	
Since words often have varied meanings and nuances, please use these definitions for reference. The author uses them throughout the book with the noted interpretation.	
Skill:	a competence due to practice, special training and/or expertise
Knowledge:	acquaintance with facts, truth, and information from study and/or experience
Perception:	the act of understanding through the senses or the mind; cognizance
World view:	working cognitive orientation / outlook; mindset
Strength:	"the ability to consistently provide near-perfect performance"**
Talent:	"a natural way of thinking, feeling or behaving"**
Competency or Ability:	the power to perform; proficiency
Ability, Capacity, Capability, Competence:	used by author interchangeably throughout the book; note that grammatically "ability" may refer to a qualitative measure of a person and "capacity" to a quantitative one.
**Definitions from Tom Rath's Strengthsfinder 2.0.	

> *There are two primary choices in life: to accept conditions as they exist, or accept the responsibility for changing them.*
>
> - Dr. Denis Waitley
> Productivity Expert

Chapter 5: Take a Stand: Own Your Career

Owning your career direction is the only opportunity you have for what used to be called "job security" and the stability of consistent work. While this takes different thinking and behaviors, you make changes by choice all the time. You change your behaviors when you buy a home or auto, when you have children or own a pet, and you can do the same with your work. When you recognize yourself and your intellect as an asset and you work consciously to invest wisely so its value increases, you have reached another milestone.

What is Career Ownership?

Career Ownership is a career model that shows you how to determine your best career path and outline a learning strategy and an alignment plan to keep you on that path. By owning your career, you can move within or among organizations, aligning your career direction with the organization's needs and doing work that is satisfying and matters to you. Owning your career is built on the concept of being an "intrepreneur," which is defined in Wikipedia as someone who "focuses on innovation and creativity." They operate within the organization's environment and derive reward and motivation from within themselves. The result is a win-win for the "intrapreneur" and the organization.

The Career Ownership Model

The Career Ownership model guides you to build a solid foundation, explore possibilities and recognize your best contributions, and make a business case or proposal for aligning your work with the strategic direction of your organization.

The model's 5 practical work areas as shown in the pyramid are best built from the bottom up:

1. Uncovering Your Personal Foundation

2. Leveraging Your Strengths

3. Learning the Organization's Direction, Values and Needs

4. Discovering Mentors and Matches

5. Making the Business Case for Your Career Direction

We'll examine each of these work areas in the next chapters so you're ready to use the worksheets and move from renting to owning your career direction.

Broad Benefits of Career Ownership

You stop waiting. You take responsibility. You no longer feel like a victim of someone else's decisions. You create strategy for a path within your current organization if it's there to be found, or you move toward another organization with a better fit.

And because so much of career ownership may be unfamiliar, the process is intentionally crafted to bolster your development of the skills and mind set you need most. Rather than increasing anxiety from yet another change, the process increases your confidence and self-efficacy. How?

- You examine your organization, its challenges, the industry and your customers through a different lens. When you do, you open your perspective to additional pieces of the economic puzzle at least partially created by a global marketplace. In exploring the bigger picture, you talk with peers, leaders and other knowledgeable folks and collaborate on common issues. This bigger picture expands your view so you identify work areas where you can make an impact. This increases your confidence and recognition of what you have to offer and how you can do it.

- The first worksheets guide you to "surface" those things that make you Authentically you: your values, motivators, innate talents, skills, etc. When you consciously see what's important to you, what drives you, what makes you tick and what frustrates you, you have a Foundation or benchmark for yourself. This in-depth self-knowledge is captivating, clear, undeniable and explains so much! Your belief-in-self translates into a broader efficacy that will drive your work direction.

- The Career Ownership process is grounded in learning: about yourself, your organization, enterprise needs, possibilities and relationships. This learning shows you how to go after what you need and reinforces what you learn in the form of relevant information to act on and the reciprocal relationships that are the basis of every economy. This learning also generates increased resilience and change-agility…skills you'll use for the rest of your life.

And the Career Ownership model intentionally encourages you to expand your world view: you can't learn new things about yourself, your work and business without experiencing and seeing things a bit differently. As noted in the last chapter, mindsets may be the greatest obstacle for most of us in moving toward change; they frequently keep us stuck. For example, if your view of "how work should be" is based upon a belief from the 20th century such as: "If I work hard and do everything my boss says, I am a valuable employee," this assumption will prevent you from taking ownership of your career direction.

> Your mindset or world view is the "lens" or "frame" through which you interpret the world. It's a set of assumptions and beliefs shaped by all of your learning and experiences. The broader your world view, the more open you are to possibilities.

Challenges

- **The biggest challenge may be your own excuses.** The voice in your head may be saying "not me," "not now," "too much work," "I'm too old for this," or, [insert excuse here]. Human beings are great at denial and at staying in the comfort zone.

Even our bodies fight change. Our bodies are created to move us toward equilibrium through homeostasis, which is the tendency of our bodies to maintain internal stability. While physiologically we need the equilibrium of homeostasis, it's also responsible for any number of diseases. The point is we often need to work against some of those things that tether us to the comfort zone. Only by getting out of your comfort place will you be able to find the stability and confidence you want from your work.

- **Few role models exist for Career Ownership.** Chances are you know people who "own" their career because they run their own businesses, but probably not many who own their careers inside an organization. Career Owners may not be prevalent now, but they soon will be. Organizations need what Career Owners contribute. Organizations want to be successful in the global economy; this means in markets where "all brains on deck" can collaborate to create that success.

Organizations know that customers value new and different products and services, and that customers return to do business where they have strong emotional connections. The only way to connect with a product or service is through a human being, the employee. And employees who use their talents to further the organization's mission are the ones that make this happen. They love what they do and ensure that customers *want* to return. While they may not be predominant now, Career Owners will be highly-valued as flexible and confident workers who can dance not only with mercurial customers, but also with industries as they change and with the economy as it travels the global market.

- **You may be intimidated by the work involved in taking ownership of your career.** Owning your career isn't an auto-pilot place; owning your career is a very intentional one. If you choose to own your career, you will learn more about yourself than you ever have before. You'll take responsibility for seeking work that fits best. You will not wait for your manager to tell you what to do, nor will you waste time on ways to look busy. You'll identify those who can mentor you, as well as identify those whom you can mentor. You'll be doing the work of a "partner" v. an "employee."

Taking career responsibility is very different than showing up from 8 to 5, doing what's in your job description, collecting your paycheck, and then heading out to live your life. Career Ownership is labor intensive yet the reward is a life of balance and work that makes a difference. Your work moves from a draining experience to an energizer that reflects your talents and values.

You can let these challenges stop you, or you can make sure they don't.

Investment

Career Ownership **will** cost you. You pay to take care of the things dear to you – your children, your home, your pet, your health. You willingly take responsibility for all of these things. Why would you leave your career to chance?

As we move from adolescence to maturity, our views about responsibility change. When we become responsible for ourselves, we understand how patience and effort allow us to preserve things we care about. We leave behind the view that someone else will take care of us.

Why not the same with your career? Today, learning and flexibility will define your economic stability.

What's the investment? We need time and money to invest in ourselves to make us marketable, but we also must make emotional and mental shifts to support our investment.

For some, the challenge is energizing and means little risk; for others, the move from dependency to ownership is so great that a guide is your best bet. If you are tentative about ownership thing, then find a coach who is certified in the Career Ownership program. Why *wouldn't* you be willing to invest in yourself to create a path that serves you for the rest of your work life?

Working through the model

The next chapters take you through each part of the model using worksheets to explore and collect relevant information. As you complete the worksheets, you'll want to reflect on your responses and look for similar "threads" or themes.

You'll find these by making note of words, ideas, or thoughts that repeat or echo in your work. You might find threads within a worksheet; you will definitely discover them when you compare worksheets. Read what Mary in the case study noted in Figure 3 has to say about themes:

Themes: Surprisingly Helpful

"As I made my way through the worksheets, I came across thoughts and dreams I'd forgotten about. Some things I put aside as being impractical or too time consuming. Some things seemed to be unrelated to any kind of work I might really do and also make a living!

Words that kept coming up over and over were "curiosity," "writing," "investigation" and "research." Try as I might, the only things that came to mind were "private detectives" or the CSI people! When I took these threads and compared them to work that needed these things, I came up with 8 or 9 possibilities. I was surprised there were so many.

While I didn't feel I was cut out to be a forensics investigator, and I didn't want to go back to school to get a law degree, I started looking into a paralegal career. It really needed all of the themes that were so true of me. Finding the themes really made a difference for me in knowing what work would be satisfying."

Mary, career coaching client

Figure 3: *Themes provide messages*

You can use the THREADS: Finding Your Life Themes worksheet as a collection point and reflection place for your findings. You'll find it following the Foundation worksheets in the next chapter.

Take aways:

1. Taking Career Ownership gives you confidence in your change-agility and in making career decisions that are right for you.

2. Taking Career Ownership is likely unexplored territory: be ready for that voice inside your head to tell you stories to try and keep you safe!

3. Career Ownership is work, but a valuable and rewarding work that uses the best of all you have to offer.

Knowing others is wisdom;
knowing yourself is Enlightenment.

- Lao Tzu
ancient Chinese philosopher

Chapter 6: Unearth Your Foundation to Reveal the Real You

Just like a home's foundation is the source of its stability, your Foundation is the source of your work and career stability and your lifelong earning power. Your Foundation is who you are and what you're about. The Foundation work makes it visible and real to you.

A building's foundation is usually hidden. The real you can be hidden, too. The real you may hide for fear of not fitting into your workplace. Maybe the real you lacks confidence. The work of Uncovering your Foundation involves discovering what's most important and at the core of your being: your values, successes, engagers or intrinsic motivators, aspirations, skills, and work climate. A most interesting thing happens the closer you get to your Foundation: your confidence grows stronger. Your restored sense of self becomes your solid ground!

As you become increasingly aware of the personal preferences that make up your Foundation, you'll find that themes emerge. Ideas and thoughts will repeat and relate to each other. These themes or threads are essential to your Foundation and are strong clues to identifying work that will satisfy you.

For some, the theme might be "outdoors;" for others, it might be something like "details" or "development." The themes clarify and reflect what is most significant to you. When you know your themes, you create the benchmark for yourself and your work decisions. Because you have a strong sense of what matters, the answers to nagging questions have clear answers:

- Why am I dissatisfied with my current job?

- What kind of work will satisfy me…will energize me every day?

- Will I be a fit with the work of a potential project?

- Is this open position a good short-term and long-term opportunity for me?

- What's my next best direction: up, lateral or out?

The increased self-awareness you'll have from uncovering your Foundation also generates self-esteem and self-efficacy. Without these you're destined to be a renter, unable or unwilling to take responsibility for making your way on your own.

Why you need it

When you know your Foundation, you can make intentional, informed career choices. Your Foundation becomes your guide, and makes decisions measurable.

When in sync with your Foundation, you can recognize how aligned or not you are with the work you do. When you can't live your values at work or you are mired in a routine without challenges, you'll be frustrated and bored. "Finding a different job" isn't the answer. Doing work that syncs with your Foundation *is*.

You will be most satisfied doing the work that includes your strongest themes. Even with a few themes identified, you can assess your current work and begin to identify the source of your frustrations or dissatisfaction. Your themes describe the career you seek and satisfying work opportunities.

Pitfalls to avoid

This all seems so basic; what might trip you up?

1. **Skipping this Foundation work because it seems banal or unnecessary.** Although you've lived in your skin for years, it's still possible to "not know" who you really are! It's easy to become a reflection of those around you and the institutions in which you live every day. Sometimes it is to the detriment of your true self. The Foundation process is an opportunity to become conscious of the pieces that make you, you. Becoming aware of the pieces in an organized process helps you identify the themes that guide smart career choices.

2. **Skipping this work because you've taken assessments in the past.** Your foundation is best understood through looking inside and becoming aware of those things that are unique to you. When you write these things and speak them out loud they become real. While assessments have value, no assessment can replace the introspection that gets to your personal truth. No electronic report allows you to get a full picture of who you are and what you're about. Assessments may add to what we know about ourselves, but they can never replace it.

3. **Skipping this work because a manager or mentor has always told you what you need.** Falling into the trap of allowing someone else to set your direction is easy. Most institutions (workplaces included) actually program us to do this. This is especially true for baby boomers because the work culture encouraged us to be passive about our careers. 'Back in the day' we knew the direction of our career through our education tracks and career ladders.

   There's no logic to placing your career satisfaction in someone else's hands. Organizations today have limited career development programs, no career ladders and measure their success by how finely they can shave expenses. Most certainly your career direction isn't on anybody's radar screen but your own.

4. **Thinking you can do this work without objective feedback.** Some of us are more comfortable with introspective work than others. If you just don't want to look inside, then it's best that you wait until you're ready.

A well-trained career coach, not a job coach, can make this introspective process productive *for you*. A career coach is an objective outside observer who can provide feedback and ask discerning questions. We all have blind spots, things we don't see in ourselves that other people do. We all have a tendency to avoid the hard questions even though answering these questions can provide us with relevant insight. Just as you would use a real-estate agent to help you locate the right home and feel confident in its structural integrity, a career coach is a smart escort through this process.

While we usually turn to our family and friends for advice, that's not a good idea here. First, they aren't objective: they care about us and want the best for us, so their advice is often based on their own world views, relevant or not. And second, an important part of the Career Ownership process is feedback and questioning, skills necessary to amplify your learning. You can easily short-change yourself by requesting assistance from someone who is uncomfortable with these skills.

These worksheets will help you surface your Foundational themes:

Worksheets: Foundation & Fit

1. **Who I Am**

2. **What I Value**

3. **What Energizes Me**

4. **What My Talents Are**

5. **Where My Skills Lie**

6. **How I Work Best**

7. **What Possibilities Fit Me**

8. **My Target Directions**

9. **THREADS: Finding My Life Themes**

It's not necessary to complete the worksheets in order although Worksheets # 1 through 6 provide valuable information for completing Worksheets # 7 and 8. You may find that a comfortable integration happens by completing the worksheets in order, especially if you process each one with a coach who can ensure that you're finding and evaluating all the clues.

It's smart to work with the THREADS worksheet after you complete each individual worksheet. Each of the Foundation worksheets and the Strengthsfinder report has a place in the THREADS worksheet, with space for noting your themes and clues. Tracking your themes as you go also encourages you to stay conscious of your themes in your work and other life activities. And your awareness will encourage you to use your Strengths more often and to noticeably observe the results.

If you prefer to work with full-size worksheets, you can download the worksheets in an 8 ½" x 11" format at www.workforcechange.com within the *Career Ownership* section, 'Member login," passcode "cobook".

Career Ownership

Self-discovery = Foundation & Fit

Foundation Worksheet: Who I Am

The process of self-discovery is one that is critical in defining your best career direction. It's through self-discovery that you're able to become clear on "who you are" and "what you're about." When you know that, you have a Foundation upon which to base decisions and direction. Using your foundation as a benchmark gives you a standard or measure that reflects you—authentically—so your decision fits you.

This worksheet asks you to examine what's significant and connected for you. It's best to go through the worksheet quickly jotting your first intuitive responses; then put it aside for a few days. Come back to it at another time to examine your responses again and clarify or revise.

1. **When you were a child, what did you want to be when you grew up? Why? If you didn't accomplish that, what got in your way?**

2. **If you had unlimited amounts of money to give away, to which cause or good work would you give…and why? List up to three.**

3. **What's your # 1 life success? What is its importance to you?**

4. **What's your # 1 work success? What is its importance to you?**

5. **What 3 words that describe you do you want chiseled on your tombstone?**

© 2009-10 CompassPoint Coaching LLC dba Workforce Change
Contact Information: Janine Moon, 614.488-6876; Janine@WorkforceChange.com
http://CareerOwners.wordpress.com

Self-discovery = **Foundation & Fit**

6. Do you have a purpose for being on this earth? If so, what is it? How do you know?

7. What are the top 5 to 7 tenets that are important for you to teach your children?

8. We often learn most by experience. What's the greatest learning you've had through just living your life?

9. If you died tomorrow, what would you regret? If you had one week to clean up your regret(s), how would you and in what order?

10. What makes you feel really great about yourself? What is it exactly that creates the feeling?

11. What are you naturally good at? (talents, skills, tasks, approaches, etc.)

12. What are you doing when you lose track of time, meal-time passes by unnoticed and you experience joy and satisfaction?

© 2009-10 CompassPoint Coaching LLC dba Workforce Change
Contact Information: Janine Moon, 614.488-6876; Janine@WorkforceChange.com
http://CareerOwners.wordpress.com

Career Ownership

Self-discovery = Foundation & Fit

13. What's holding you back from going after your dreams? (practical, emotional or otherwise)

14. Consider the world, society, your community and your family. What does each need from you that only you can provide?

15. Describe how you are when you are being (as opposed to doing).

From these responses, consider this:

Describe what is true about you that you've learned or relearned through this activity. Put your thoughts in the box

Career Ownership

Self-discovery = Foundation & Fit

Foundation Worksheet: What I Value

The process of self-discovery is one that is critical in defining your best career direction. It's through self-discovery that you're able to become clear on "who you are" and "what you're about." When you know that, you have a Foundation upon which to base decisions and direction. Using your foundation as a benchmark gives you a standard or measure that reflects you—authentically—so your decision fits you.

This worksheet asks you to examine your values—the things that really matter to you. These are usually beliefs, ideas, principles, or qualities that we hold as sacred or in very high regard. You need to "live" your values or you will encounter frustration and significant stress. This worksheet will help you "surface" and become aware of those values that are dear to you. Recognizing and living your core values is the very basis for work and career satisfaction. In this worksheet, you are asked to identify those values that are most important or core to you; defining these does not negate other values.

Find a quiet place to complete this worksheet, and listen to your intuition and inner conversation as you complete your selections. Review the words listed, and identify those that are very important to you. (The blanks allow you to include values that this list may have missed.) Now, narrow your list to your top 10.

Core Values

Peace	Courage	Respect	Love
Wealth	Wisdom	Success	Integrity
Family	Equality	Happiness	Power
Influence	Recognition	Friendship	Status
Joy	Growth	Freedom	Stability
Independence	Contribution	Accomplishment	Spirituality

Career Ownership

Self-discovery = Foundation & Fit

When you have your top 10, write each in a box in the Values Column. Then, write each in the same order in a box at the top of each column. Now, measure each against the others, one at a time. As you compare two values, write the more important of the two in the white grid box where the two values meet. For example, in the top corner white block you'll write the more important of your values, # 1 or # 10.

Values	1	2	3	4	5	6	7	8	9	10
1										
2										
3										
4										
5										
6										
7										
8										
9										
10										

Which of your values received the most "votes"? List your top 3 here:

Just looking at your top 3, do they feel right to you? Is there another one on the list that you feel should be in the top 3 but didn't make the vote cut?

Which of your top 3 values can you live each day in your work? Note 2 examples of how you have recently acted on each value.

Are you unable to act on any of your top 3 at work? If so, note an example or two.

Reminder: place your values on the THREADS worksheet!

Career Ownership

Self-discovery = Foundation & Fit

Foundation Worksheet: What Energizes Me

The process of self-discovery is one that is critical in defining your best career direction. It's through self-discovery that you're able to become clear on "who you are" and "what you're about." When you know that, you have a Foundation upon which to base decisions and direction. Using your foundation as a benchmark gives you a standard or measure that reflects you—authentically—so your decision fits you.

This worksheet asks you to examine your sources of energy and the things that engage you. You do things and take actions because you have internal (intrinsic) needs to fill. Your work can help fill needs, starve them, or possibly some of both. The more your needs are filled through your work, the more committed, proactive and productive you will be. Respond to each of the statements below, providing a brief explanation for each.

1. What group or club did you last join voluntarily? Why?

2. Of what work success (in your current position) are you most proud? To what do you attribute your success? What other successes make you smile?

3. When have you successfully been able to lead a group or team or unit of people? How do you account for your success?

4. What is your favorite way to learn? What learning path have you been on for the last 1-3 years?

5. What kind of work would you do for free? What would be its value to you?

6. In what most recent event have you participated where you were motivated to do or be your best? Describe the event and your participation in it.

7. Identify 3 times in your life where you were so energized about something that you couldn't wait to get started, you loved every minute you were engaged, and you hated to see those times end. What do the 3 times have in common?

8. Consider these 8 "motivation and engagement" themes. Now look at your answers for each of the 7 questions above. For each event or activity you have described, identify which of these 8 themes is most prominently reflected in your responses. You might have a single theme or more than one for your responses.

Relationships   Autonomy

Social Status/Esteem   Goal-focused

Achievement   Growth/Self-actualization

Power/Influence   Thrill

My top 3 Motivation & Engagement themes

Reminder: place your energizers on the THREADS worksheet!

 Career Ownership

Self-discovery = Foundation & Fit

Foundation Worksheet: What My Talents Are

The process of self-discovery is one that is critical in defining your best career direction. It's through self-discovery that you're able to become clear on "who you are" and "what you're about." When you know that, you have a Foundation upon which to base decisions and direction. Using your foundation as a benchmark gives you a standard or measure that reflects you—authentically—so your decision fits you.

This worksheet asks you to examine your talents and the strengths into which you have developed those talents. Look at these definitions:

Talent: "a natural way of thinking, feeling, behaving"[1]

Strength: "the ability to consistently provide near perfect performance"[2]

While we are most often encouraged to "fix our weaknesses" or "focus on areas for improvement," our potential for personal and professional growth is strongest when we can work on what we do well, v. what we don't. This strengths focus also helps us examine our mindset, and can shift or strengthen ours from "fixed" to "growth."[3] And a growth mindset is the source of our success.

Mindsets: **Fixed** & **Growth**

 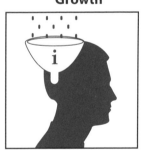

Check your mindsets: Over the next five days, be aware of your mindsets at work, home and other places. Make notes on where and when your mind is closed (Fixed) or open (Growth).

Events: _____

Projects: _____

People (you are with): _____

Career Ownership
Self-discovery = Foundation & Fit

Talents: list your 5 identified through the Strengthsfinder 2.0 assessment.

_____   _____

_____   _____

_____

Tracking your talents: Write each of your talents on one of the lines below. In the space by each talent, track your display of that talent over a week and note your observations. Describe the situation, the people you were with, how you utilized the talent, and the outcome(s).

Talent or Strength	How I display it	Yes/No (Could I leverage this strength into a Growth mindset?)
1.		
2.		
3.		
4.		
5.		

Reminder: place your strengths on the THREADS worksheet!

[1,2] Rath, Tom. Strengthsfinder 2.0. 2007. Gallup Press.
[3] Dweck, Carol S. Mindset: The New Psychology of Success. 2006. Ballantine Books.

Foundation Worksheet: Where My Skills Lie

The process of self-discovery is one that is critical in defining your best career direction. It's through self-discovery that you're able to become clear on "who you are" and "what you're about." When you know that, you have a Foundation upon which to base decisions and direction. Using your foundation as a benchmark gives you a standard or measure that reflects you—authentically—so your decision fits you.

In reviewing your skills, you're asked to take a broader look than you normally might. You do, of course, have job-related and/or profession-related skills. In addition, you're asked to note your people or "interpersonal" skills, your "business" skills and your "personal effectiveness" skills. For each section, identify or check your individual skill, a measure of it (e.g. pro, newbie, solid, etc.) and an example of your use of that skill.

Section 1: Job-related and Profession-related Skills

Job/Profession: _____

List those skills that are technically and/or professionally necessary for you to do your work. (For example, you might list things like legal research; project tools; site design; use of codes and regulations; CRM system use; facilitation skills; etc.)

Skill	Example(s)
1.	
2.	
3.	
4.	
5.	
6.	
7.	
8.	
9.	
10.	

Career Ownership

Self-discovery = Foundation & Fit

Section 2: Interpersonal (Emotional Intelligence) Skills

Identify your use of any of these skills, making note of an example.

Leadership

Visioning

Adapting

Engaging

Developing others

Change-ability/agility

Other:

Communication

Writing

Speaking

Relationship building

Influencing

Collaboration/Conflict Management

Other:

Section 3: Business Skills

Identify your use of any of these skills, making note of an example.

Problem-solving

Critical thinking

Strategic thinking

Problem-solving tools (SWOT, Lateral, Force Field Analysis, etc.)

Industry and Organization-relevant

Industry innovations

Customer expectations/relationships

Competitor business models

Financial Analysis

Career Ownership

Self-discovery = Foundation & Fit

Mission and strategy

Business development (goals and objectives)

Section 4: Personal effectiveness (Emotional Intelligence) Skills

Identify your level (excellent, good, fair, poor) in each of these skill areas, making note of an example.

Flexibility/Adaptability

Resilience

Stress management

Initiative

Empathy

Self-confidence

Achievement-orientation

Trustworthiness

Identify the skills you use often	Identify your strongest skills	Identify skills for development

Reminder: place your skills on the THREADS worksheet!

Career Ownership

Self-discovery = Foundation & Fit

Fit Worksheet: How I Work Best

> The process of self-discovery is one that is critical in defining your best career direction. It's through self-discovery that you're able to become clear on "who you are" and "what you're about." When you know that, you have a Foundation upon which to base decisions and direction. Using your foundation as a benchmark gives you a standard or measure that reflects you—authentically—so your [career] decisions fits you.

This worksheet helps you examine the contexts in which you work most effectively. It may mean noise or silence; independence or collaboration. What surroundings do you need to do your best work?

Contexts to consider:

Space: Describe your most productive work space. Is it large or cozy? Is it out or in? Is it plain or creatively designed? How does your space impact your effectiveness?

Cultural: Do you thrive in your current work culture, the "how we do things around here" expectations and unwritten rules? What about the culture do you find helpful, reasonable, supportive optimistic, trusting and energizing? Identify those things below. If any of the expectations or rules get in the way of you doing your best work, note them below, too.

Work processes: What workplace processes support you in doing your best work? What processes, when improved, will increase your efficiency and/or productivity? [Note: these may be project-related processes or employment-related processes.]

Do you work best in a group? Alone? Some combination?

Management: Do you get the right amount of support, recognition, information, contact, encouragement, development, and resources from your manager? From project leads? From your organization's leadership? If so, please note why; if not, please note what's missing that would improve your work results.

Career Ownership

Self-discovery = Foundation & Fit

Below are 6 descriptors of work environments.[1] Please rank order (1 being highest) your preference for the environments. Don't worry about a "correct" definition for any of them…go with what you know.

_____ realistic

_____ investigative

_____ artistic

_____ social

_____ enterprising

_____ conventional

Does your current work environment "work" for you? Are your preferred work environments reflected in your current organization? How, or not?

Reminder: place your context on the THREADS worksheet!

[1] Dr. John Holland, Ph.D. Self-directed Search. Web: http://self-directed-search.com

Career Ownership
Self-discovery = Foundation & Fit

Fit Worksheet: What Possibilities Fit Me

> The process of self-discovery is one that is critical in defining your best career direction. It's through self-discovery that you're able to become clear on "who you are" and "what you're about." When you know that, you have a Foundation upon which to base decisions and direction. Using your foundation as a benchmark gives you a standard or measure that reflects you—authentically—so your [career] decisions fit you.

This worksheet asks you to research opportunities that fit your Foundation. You have various approaches to this research, so you can examine possibilities from many directions. If you find possibility-thinking fun, you will enjoy this exercise. If you have limited experience in exploring possibilities, you may find this exercise a bit challenging. When you've completed this worksheet, you will have a list of at least 5-7 career steps/possibilities that align with who you are and what you're about. Use the Identifying Targets Worksheet to collect information.

Internet research:

Visit these sites and spend several hours during several sittings looking through work areas that align with your current industry and other industries of interest. Identify those professions or jobs or work areas that are interesting to you and fit with your Foundation findings.

The Occupational Outlook Handbook, 2008-2009 edition:
http://www.bls.gov/OCO
Also: http://www.bls.gov/oco/ocos005.htm

O*Net: http://online.onetcenter.org

Career Resource Library: http://www.acinet.org/acinet/crl/library.aspx

Career Voyages:
http://www.careervoyages.gov/construction-main.cfm

Bureau of Labor Statistics Employment Projections:
http://www.bls.gov/emp

 Career Ownership

Self-discovery = Foundation & Fit

Industry & Organization research:

1. List any industry trade and professional organizations that are relevant to your business and professional interests. If you're researching industries outside of your present one, then research organizations associated with each industry. Identify at least one industry association and one professional association.

List, also, the state and/or local chapters of any national association.

Industry Association(s) and contact information:

Professional Association(s) and contact information:

Now, contact each association you've listed and find out what career information is available. Some will have career path information, training and education opportunities, job descriptions of industry positions, and professionals and leaders in the industry available to talk about career opportunities. Ask specifically for information/guidance on any of the "possibilities" you identified in your online career research.

2. List everyone associated with an industry of interest that might be willing to talk with you about careers in the industry and their organization. These might be project managers, experienced peers, a long-time associate, someone who has mentored you, as well as your manager. For those industries of greatest interest, arrange for a telephone or in-person discussion or an informational interview. Ask any questions (below) that apply, and take notes on the Identifying Targets Worksheet:

•Knowing me and my work, what career directions might be good for me and why?

•If my interests lie in xxx direction, what informal learning opportunities can you suggest?

•How could I best become ready for my next career move?

•Would you be willing to let me shadow you to better understand _____ (the work done by the individual)?

•What do you like about _____ (work)? What are the down-sides to it?

•What are the growth projections for your field?

•What suggestions do you have for me so that I can keep growing and developing as an individual and improve my contributions to the company? (current organization)

© 2009-10 CompassPoint Coaching LLC dba Workforce Change
Contact Information: Janine Moon, 614.488-6876; Janine@WorkforceChange.com
http://CareerOwners.wordpress.com

Career Ownership

Self-discovery = Foundation & Fit

Fit Worksheet: Identifying Targets

The process of self-discovery is one that is critical in defining your best career direction. It's through self-discovery that you're able to become clear on "who you are" and "what you're about." When you know that, you have a Foundation upon which to base decisions and direction. Using your foundation as a benchmark gives you a standard or measure that reflects you—authentically—so your [career] decisions fits you.

The worksheet on the following page helps you collect information on possible work and career directions. As you examine possibilities and talk with people, note your findings on this worksheet for easy reference.

Given your research so far, what direction(s) are most interesting to you? Which direction(s) line up with the information you have from the Foundation work sheets?

WHO will you discuss this with to test your ideas and potential direction? Name _____

NOW......... consider the line below to be your career path over the next 3 years. Plot along the line thoughts, ideas, learning opportunities, suggestions and possibilities you have identified in your work so far!

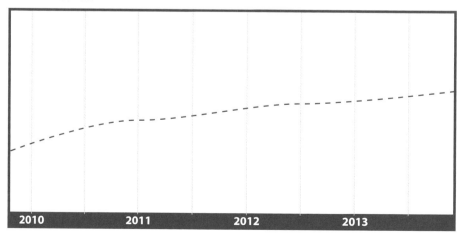

2010   2011   2012   2013

© 2009-10 CompassPoint Coaching LLC dba Workforce Change
Contact Information: Janine Moon, 614.488-6876; Janine@WorkforceChange.com
http://CareerOwners.wordpress.com

Career Ownership

Self-discovery = Foundation & Fit

Source	Findings, Clues, Information, Discoveries, Conclusions
Your current thoughts, ideas	
Findings from internet research, career sites	
Current Industry (and other Industries of interest) sources	
Professional Association sources	
Discussions with current employer managers, leaders and associates	

Career Ownership

Self-discovery = Foundation & Fit

THREADS: Finding Your Life Themes

Worksheets	Who	Values	Energy	Talents	Strengths	Skills	Context	Possibilities, Targets	Consistent Themes
Who I Am									
What I Value									
What Energizes Me									
What my Talents Are (Worksheet)									
Strengths (from Strengthfinder 2.0)									

THREADS: Finding Your Life Themes

Worksheets	Who	Values	Energy	Talents	Strengths	Skills	Context	Possibilities, Targets	Consistent Themes
Where My Skills Lie									
How I Work Best / Context									
Possibilities & Targets Clues									
Other Observations or Threads									
Summaries: words, thoughts, a-ha moments!									

> *Whatever you are from nature, keep to it; never desert your own line of talent...Be what Nature intended you for, and you will succeed.*
>
> - Sydney Smith
> English Essayist

Chapter 7: Find Your Strengths and Flex Your Muscles

Leveraging your Strengths—more accurately described as Talents—is critical to your work satisfaction and the contribution you make to an organization. Your innate Strengths are not necessarily the same as skills, and they're also something not often discussed. But over the last 20 years, much has been written about Strengths and the contribution they make in doing your best work.

Strengths, according to the work of The Gallup Organization, Marcus Buckingham and others, stem from innate talents. Talents are natural abilities, unique to each individual. Even if we share a particular Strength, we hold it in different capacities. We are born with these natural abilities that may be behavioral or cognitive, and we excel at them. In fact, our talents often show themselves as capabilities that we take so much for granted we think everyone can do them, as effortlessly and naturally as we do. As a result we often undervalue our strengths and ignore them, going through life without knowing we have such genius.

The most often heard comment from people who learn their strengths is "I didn't know what to call this!" or "Now I understand why [doing something] is so easy!"

The revelation of identifying your natural strengths is often eye-opening and a real boost to self-esteem. Many of us lived in families and attended schools whose cultures taught modesty and humility as the proper ways to be. We were focused on our weaknesses and our limitations, and taught to work on improving them. While we might have heard about a strength, it was likely in the context of academics or sports: never by itself and never with the thought that it could be a powerful life-long advantage.

Beginning in the 1960s, the Gallup Organization began collecting information from millions of respondents on 34 *strengths*, defined as behaviors, feelings or thoughts that occur naturally in us. The online assessments, *The Clifton Strengths Finder* and the more recent *Strengthsfinder 2.0* provide a report identifying the taker's top five talents. Even with the millions of individuals who have taken the assessments, the results are highly customized considering not only top five strengths but the order of their priority and their relationship to each other.

Examples of Gallup's 34 Strengths:
Arranger • Belief • Context • Strategic • Communication
Ideation • Empathy • Focus • Significance • Woo • Input

Why should you care? Because working from your Strengths is a positive and productive way to work: you are committed to and engaged in what you're doing, and your intrinsic motivation (factors like challenge, mastery and curiosity) is tapped. Gallup's work continues to show that when people focus on their strengths every day, they report high work satisfaction and quality of life.

Begin with the assessment: go to www.stregthsfinder.com, take the online Strengthsfinder assessment and you'll receive a report that identifies your top 5 strengths. The report also includes application and developmental information for you to build upon your strengths. When you can identify your top strengths and analyze how you use them—or not—in your work, you get another piece of your Foundation puzzle. Using your strengths in your work every day increases your self-efficacy and that translates to better contributions: to your customers and to your own motivation.

Increasing your awareness of your Strengths, how you use them at work, and how you might leverage them to improve results for you and your organization outcomes is the purpose of this chapter's worksheets. Each of the worksheets asks you to focus on better recognizing and using your strengths consciously, frequently and generously towards a stronger personal and professional you.

Pitfalls to Avoid

Getting familiar with your strengths makes a lot of sense; what could possibly get in your way?

1. **Diminishing the importance of strengths-based work.** You might think, "I know what I'm good at," or "Focusing on improving makes more sense to me." You probably do know what you're good at—but that doesn't mean you recognize your Strengths. And like many things, if you don't recognize your Strengths, you can't intentionally use them.

   Leveraging your Strengths at work gives you the best conditions for really caring about the outcomes, making contributions to the organization, increasing your sense of mastery and purpose and knowing—with certainty—that you provide value.

2. **Expecting that everyone knows their Strengths and uses them.** Many don't know their Strengths unless the organization has a Strengths-based culture. You have the opportunity to lead your team, your department, and your project partners toward more productive outcomes by introducing them to Strengths-thinking. You'll find a number of suggestions for 'how to use' your Strengths in your Strengthsfinder report.

The worksheets following help you focus your Strengths by tracking when and how you use them, and understanding their impact on your successes. You additionally might talk with people who know you well and collect their observations. When you've finished with your Strengths work, be sure to add relevant clues and ideas to your THREADS worksheet.

Career Ownership

Strengths = Talent + Effort

Strengths Worksheet: My Talents and How I Use Them

> In a world where we are expected to focus on 'fixing our weaknesses,' learning to leverage our strengths is application of unparalleled development. When we utilize our strengths, we are using our gift to a state of perfection. We become so lost in the work that it isn't like work at all, because our strength makes it easy and time-less.

This worksheet is to increase your awareness of those activities that come easily to you, so that your awareness leads you to doing more of the work that uses your innate talents. As you learn your strengths and how to leverage them, your productivity increases, you struggle less, and your emotional commitment to the work you do heightens your contribution and provides the greater satisfaction.

Using your Strengthsfinder 2.0 report, list your top 5 strengths in the first column. Two additional boxes are included so you can add additional strengths that didn't make the top 5 but that you feel apply to you. In the second column, write a practical application of the strength as you have used it. Use the last column to track your use of that talent/strength over the next 7 days.

Talent Themes	Application (past)	Application (current)
1.		
2.		

Career Ownership

Strengths = Talent + Effort

Talent Themes	Application (past)	Application (current)
3.		
4.		
5.		
6.		
7.		

Career Ownership

Strengths = Talent + Effort

Consider these questions:

1. Which two of your themes are most prevalent in your work? Do you use those strengths every day?

2. Where and when do you use them in your work?

3. Do these themes focus on relationships, thoughts, goals or affecting something or someone?

4. How might these two themes complement each other?

Career Ownership

Strengths = Talent + Effort

Strengths Worksheet: Themes and Success

In a world where we are expected to focus on 'fixing our weaknesses,' learning to leverage our strengths is application of unparalleled development. When we utilize our strengths, we are using our gift to a state of perfection. We become so lost in the work that it isn't like work at all, because our strength makes it easy and time-less.

This worksheet allows you to examine your two greatest successes in order to recognize how you used your talents in accomplishing those achievements.

Success #1 (work)		
Which talent was critical? Describe it, i.e. how you used the talent.	**Which talent was critical? Describe it, i.e. how you used the talent.**	**Which talent was critical? Describe it, i.e. how you used the talent.**

Career Ownership

Strengths = Talent + Effort

Success #2 (not work)		
Which talent was critical? Describe it, i.e. how you used the talent.	**Which talent was critical? Describe it, i.e. how you used the talent.**	**Which talent was critical? Describe it, i.e. how you used the talent.**

Name a work-related challenge you're currently facing:

How could you leverage one or more of the talents you noted above to respond to it? List 3 or 4 actions or applications you could consider.

© 2009-10 CompassPoint Coaching LLC dba Workforce Change
Contact Information: Janine Moon, 614.488-6876; Janine@WorkforceChange.com
http://CareerOwners.wordpress.com

Career Ownership

Strengths = Talent + Effort

Strengths Worksheet: How Others See Your Talents

In a world where we are expected to focus on 'fixing our weaknesses,' learning to leverage our strengths is application of unparalleled development. When we utilize our strengths, we are using our gift to a state of perfection. We become so lost in the work that it isn't like work at all, because our strength makes it easy and time-less.

This worksheet gives you the opportunity to understand how others recognize your talent themes and what they see and hear when you use your strengths.

1. **Preparation**

   Review again the description of each of your 5 strengths, underlining or highlighting all words that resonate with you…those that ring very true. Add to each of the descriptions any examples that come to mind of you using that talent in your work or play activities. Brief notes are good.

2. **Activity**

   Contact four people who know you well, friends or family or colleagues. One at a time, read each of your 5 strengths and their descriptions to each person. As you read a description, ask these questions and note the answers they give you.

   1. On a scale of 1-5, [5 is High and 1 is Low], how well does this describe me? Which of the words or phrases in the description are particularly accurate? (List 3-5)

   2. Would you give me an example or two of when you have observed or heard me use the strength? What does it look like, sound like, feel like in a situation or conversation?

Note your responses in the table on the next page.

Career Ownership

Strengths = Talent + Effort

Strength	Name:	Name:	Name:	Name:
1.				
2.				
3.				
4.				
5.				

Rank your themes from "most recognized" to "least recognized" by the people you interviewed.

1.

2.

3.

4.

5.

Is this information plausible? Does it align with your own knowledge around your **themes?**

I feel sorry for the person who can't get genuinely excited about his work. Not only will he never be satisfied, but he will never achieve anything worthwhile.

- Walter Chrysler
Founder of Chrysler

Chapter 8: Discover Your Career Customer... the Organization

Some of the most important work you'll do is developing targeted work areas within your organization. Without developing these targets, you may miss opportunities or follow misguided advice. Worse yet, you may think that the only openings are those posted as "jobs"... and you would be wrong!

Organizations today have a tremendous amount of work to be done that doesn't always fit nicely into job boxes. There are headcount issues. And budget issues. And expense curtailment programs. But the work is still there even though no "jobs" are posted. And it's this work that you're looking to uncover!

The research you'll do examines your organization from both the big picture and the detailed views. From a big picture view, you need to know the growth directions of your organization, of course, but also its strategies and competitors. What do financial reports, annual reports and other reports for the last few years indicate? Who are your best customers and what are their satisfaction scores? What sales and marketing strategies are in play? Where are change programs driving innovation? What projects get funding?

From a smaller perspective, what politics drive decisions? Who are the people who know what's happening? Who are the connectors? These folks may not be in high-level positions, but they serve as a nexus for company information. What's the future of your current department or enterprise? Is it growing or shrinking?

Knowing the answers to these questions will prevent you from being blindsided—by a layoff or staff changes or shifts in role responsibilities. It will take you beyond the partitions of your cubicle to get a trued-up view of your company's business reality. **This work will identify the directions where you can provide the most value.** And, that's the mother lode of this research.

Panning for gold

Anything worth having takes some work. When you begin planning a home purchase, you consider location and then you research: comparable homes and selling prices, neighborhood property values and even the school system, so you have information that will help you make a wise decision. You search for property and tax records, visit surrounding neighborhoods and evaluate community resources. Researching your organization is much the same.

Take a look at the parallels:

When buying a home you consider:	When researching an organization, consider:
Location, Location, Location	Mission–critical areas that parallel your foundation
Comparable homes and selling prices	Equitable qualitative and quantitative compensation of value to you
Property values	Professional and business growth potential
Infrastructure	Strategy, Leadership and Talent
Community resources	Ongoing professional development; a culture of empowerment

You may need to do some digging to find relevant information. You'll need the courage to have a straightforward response whenever someone you ask says "Why do you need that?" You'll need some creativity to go after information that seems to be out of your reach. You'll also need to become well-acquainted with those "connectors" noted above.

How you'll use what you find

You'll likely be doing this research once you've defined your Foundation. You will be clear on the capabilities that define you as a valuable asset to the company. As you explore your organization's growth directions and strategies that require the value you bring, you begin to define potential matches.

When house hunting, you know your needs and only consider homes that fit: things like size, space, and neighborhood. In your organization, consider those work areas that have the projects, substance or strategic initiatives that fit with your Foundation, i.e. your values, motivators, skills, etc. Remember: you're not so much looking for "jobs" as you are "fit:" an alignment of your "capital" with your organization's current and future market course.

Why you need this

1. Because one person (you) can identify your best work and career direction more effectively and accurately than anyone else.

2. Because you have the vision and the moxy to increase your value to your organization when no one else can see it.

3. Because organizations need 'partners' for success in today's economy, not 'employees' with traditional employee behaviors and beliefs.

4. Because partners use business capital to sustain excellence and spark growth: they collaborate, contribute and share risk and reward.

5. Because you own the 'capital' for success in your organization: you have the brains and the heart and the spirit that drives an information economy. To make wise decisions about how to use your capital, you must learn about your partner organization.

Pitfalls to avoid

- **Thinking that once is enough.** Most neighborhood profiles change in small ways over a long period of time; organizations used to be that way, too. With global competitors and shifting economics, businesses are in cycles of change that seldom slow. For you to know your organization's landscape and growth directions, you must collect intelligence on a regular basis.

- **Relying on a single source or two for your research.** This is where your connectors become very important because they are folks who are hubs for critical information, direction, changes and political currents. Connectors exist in all areas of your organization, at all levels and do all sorts of work. Connectors are people "in the know" usually before information makes its way down the hierarchy.

It's smart career strategy to identify connectors, get to know them, and build a relationship. Ask about their goals, their families, their interests and their work. Then, figure out how you can help them. The best and strongest relationships are built on mutual give and take: learn how to do this and become a role model for smart collaboration within your organization.

Mentors, too, can be great sources of information, especially if you seek mentoring relationships in various areas of the organization from people of different experience and skill levels. We'll discuss more about mentors in the next chapter.

The more facts you collect and the more perspectives you have, the better able you are to determine career opportunities that increase your value to the organization. And crafting a "win-win" career proposal only happens when you know the lay of the land: you shape a compelling business case for both you and the organization.

The worksheets following help you begin to learn your organization by suggesting information to research and how you might use it as you construct a business case. Because every organization is unique, the worksheets will likely not include all relevant information: you'll begin to recognize useful data and networks as you go.

Career Ownership
Learning the Organization

Learning the Organization: What's the Big Picture?
Examining Potential—like an Owner

Why look at the big picture? So you can stabilize your career and, in turn, your future. When you recognize the challenges of a global economy and take responsibility for contributing to business strategies, you create the opportunities to do work that makes a difference to you and the organization. That magnifies your value and ensures your ongoing satisfaction.

What you need:

_____ Company mission, strategies, business plan

_____ Trickle-down company imperatives: new directions and initiatives that will or are affecting all areas of the organization

_____ Company and (your specific) enterprise financial statements for current and past year (P&L)

_____ Your enterprise (or department) business plan for current and future years

_____ Customer service feedback reports from last several years

_____ Problematic enterprise areas and most successful enterprise areas

_____ Industry information: direction, innovations, global market impacts

_____ Competitor information: who? How does your organization stay competitive?

How to get information:

* search online: web site, press releases, Google searches, industry and competitor sites

* talk with your manager and leadership

* talk with connectors, mentors and cross-functional contacts especially those in business development and in sales and marketing

© 2009-10 CompassPoint Coaching LLC dba Workforce Change
Contact Information: Janine Moon, 614.488-6876; Janine@WorkforceChange.com
http://CareerOwners.wordpress.com

Career Ownership

Learning the Organization

What to do with the information you collect:

- analyze the information and apply your critical thinking skills: if you were an owner in the business, what are the strongest business areas and which are not? You might even do your own SWOT (Strengths, Weaknesses, Opportunities, Threats) analysis to define where any holes might be in your information. Where are risks?

- identify the strongest enterprise areas and directions for the next 1-3 years. You may already be in one of them, and your analysis may identify other potential development and/or career directions. You're looking for the best opportunities to contribute to organization growth, to align with the business direction.

- when you have a solid perspective on your Foundation, you can begin to overlay your value and contributions to organization strategies. These are the matches you'll ultimately make in the next chapters.

Note your findings in the table below; what are you missing?

Strategic Direction(s)	Enterprise / Growth Area	Collected Wisdom	Other Information

 Career Ownership

Learning the Organization

1. If you were an owner, into what area would you put your money?

2. Who has to be on-board with this to make it happen?

Notes:

Thinking like an external consultant will serve you well as you begin to analyze how your direction could align with the organization's mission and strategy.

The job of a consultant is to turn over challenges in the business (often one she doesn't know) and propose how her program, answer, or approach can help solve the challenge. When the consultant clearly defines benefits and value that the client desires, she will land the contract.

When the value isn't clear, the client says 'no' and the consultant continues looking for a better client match with her services and product offerings.

As a Career Owner, you're doing the same thing. You're looking for that business area that needs what you offer. When you develop a proposal for a career step that benefits the 'client' and provides clear value, you have a great opportunity to get the work. If you don't demonstrate the benefit, you'll need to keep looking for that better alignment and stronger proposal.

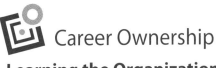

Career Ownership

Learning the Organization

Considering growth areas: Smaller Picture Realities

Why look at the smaller picture for potential growth areas? Because you must have enough support to make a case for your proposal and career direction. Whether you're planning to leverage existing enterprise needs or create a new opportunity, you must develop a proposal that includes compelling information.

When turning over opportunities or developing them, you must learn to think like a decision maker or an owner. Begin thinking about your 'case' from a marketing perspective: what do the decision makers need to know in order to say 'yes'?

Consider the following information, knowing that you may use it to analyze your proposal, to craft it or to support it.

1. **What are the future need(s) of your interest area? This might include information, demographics, analysis, etc.**

2. **What benefits and outcomes have been achieved with similar areas?**

3. **What benefits and outcomes can be anticipated with this growth area?**

4. **Have there been failures in similar areas? How would this growth area be different?**

5. **What levels of resources would be needed to achieve the anticipated outcomes?**

6. **What risks and rewards must be considered?**

Now use the table following to get the 'smaller picture' of one of your potential interest areas. Complete one table for each interest area.

Career Ownership

Learning the Organization

Growth area: _____

Smaller Picture	What will demonstrate this?	Where and from whom do I get what I need?	When and how will I approach them?
What are the needs for this growth area?			
What are tangible benefits and outcomes from current /similar areas?			
What are anticipated future outcomes and benefits from this growth area?			
Risks of this growth area			
What resources are needed to achieve the anticipated outcomes?			

> *Success depends on the support of other people.*
> *The only hurdle between you and what you want*
> *to be is in the support of other people.*
>
> - David Joseph Schwartz
> Professor and Authority on Motivation

Chapter 9: Stop Waiting to be Picked...
Find Your Mentors

Collaboration is a wonderful thing: the outcome is always 1+1= 3 or 5 or 10. As individuals, we can collect information and we can analyze it; but working alone, we cannot evaluate from any view other than our own. Our own view always has "blind" spots. Based upon our experiences, relationships, background and beliefs we have developed our world view over time, and it works to keep us comfortable. Sometimes that means not seeing things others can.

There are times that we benefit from being comfortable, but when we are examining career direction and possibilities, that comfort zone will almost surely get in our way. At the very time we need to recognize multiple options to make career head-way, our world view will keep us small. Outside perspectives from mentors, sponsors, and other objective observers are critical as we examine work possibilities.

Mentoring is a learning relationship, and seeking a mentor means you want new knowledge or insights or skills. Mentoring is an informal way to ensure you continue lifelong learning. When you work with mentors inside your organization, you can also reap the benefit of political perspective. As we use it in Career Ownership, mentoring is a relationship where both mentors and mentees benefit:

> **Mentors are people you seek out and approach for professional development. You do so with a specific scope in mind and with a willingness to be responsible for a "win-win" relationship.**
> **The more diverse your mentors, the more their perspectives challenge your thinking and expand your world.**

Why you need mentors

Finding mentors is a way for you to tailor your learning along your professional development path. While a mentor cannot replace a college degree or certification program, he or she can teach you one-on-one things not available in a formal setting. A mentor can articulate the unspoken rules in an organization or profession.

- Wondering how to navigate the politics to network in an area outside your own? A mentor can help you accomplish that.

- Want to interpret the organization's strategies to better identify opportunities? A mentor will help with that.

- Want to learn how to get over being tongue-tied with a leader in your company? A mentor can show you how.

- Want someone to tell you how they see your talents and how you can best leverage them? A mentor will give you this feedback.

- Want to know how you can approach your manager about a career discussion? Ask your mentor.

- Want to brainstorm professional growth opportunities? Ask a mentor.

- Want to learn how to ask for feedback? Work with your mentor.

- Looking to improve your critical thinking skills? Talk with your mentor.

- Looking for a different perspective of your company's challenges and opportunities? A mentor can provide that.

As you develop a positive relationship, your mentor can help open your thinking to include diverse views and possibilities. This, in turn, expands critical thinking and relationship skills needed by every enterprise: flexibility, change-agility, resilience, interpersonal skills, collaboration and confidence. One of the toughest things to recognize is what we don't know. [After all, how can you know something if you don't know it?] Your mentor can help you recognize and decrease your blind spots, that, in turn, increases your effectiveness and value.

Some mentoring relationships last for years, while others last for a few months or even a meeting or two. Clearly stating what you want to learn from a mentor will help you propose a realistic timeframe. The real key is to make sure that you create a structure that sets boundaries, recognizes the needs of the mentor, and makes the best use of time for both of you. When you've identified potential mentors, use the worksheets to develop your plan and your approach.

Mentors inside your organization who are from different functional areas or enterprises than your own are excellent sounding boards for potential career opportunities. You have nothing to lose by asking them how to approach your career interests, who to talk to, what minefields to avoid, and how to best be considered for potential openings.

Mentors can provide you with introductions to others and can open doors for additional learning opportunities: a special project, short-term shadowing, or time in another area of the organization. And, when they get to know your talents and value proposition, they can scout for potential matches within the organization. Recognizing your Strengths, your values and how you might contribute, your mentors' perspectives can provide suggestions that you may never have considered. Objective views almost always offer possibilities that we ourselves cannot see—those blind spots again!

With your mentors' guidance and your list of matches, you are in a good position to prepare a business case for your chosen career direction. Your mentors can help you define the best strategy for your approach: who to talk with, smart timing, how to present yourself and the organization path(s) that needs what you offer. Their support can be invaluable by speaking on your behalf to decision makers, helping you uncover obstacles and overcome them, and showcasing your talents within the organization.

Pitfalls to avoid

1. **Being misguided by an outdated definition of mentoring.** Traditionally, mentoring relationship were initiated by older and more experienced people who chose to tap young "up and comers," those whom the mentors deemed worthy of being brought along into an inner circle of knowledge and contacts. Young folks who were lucky enough to catch a seasoned professional's eye received mentoring. The unlucky ones did not. Don't be fooled…**mentoring doesn't work that way anymore!**

   Here's what you need to know:

   - Much mentoring is done by younger people who have tremendous skills and knowledge to share;

   - It's your choice to define yourself as an "up and comer;" waiting for someone else to do it only ages you;

   - While "inner circles" still exist, plenty of other opportunities for learning and connecting exist as well. Go find those opportunities!

   - "Waiting to be picked" for career development is how things were done in the last century when hierarchies were fat, the pace of organizations was slow and the marketplace was stable.

   - Waiting today gets you nowhere.

2. **Listening to self-doubt about your worthiness to be mentored.** Now that you know you can identify your own mentors, the voice in your head will be telling you stories. Here's one:

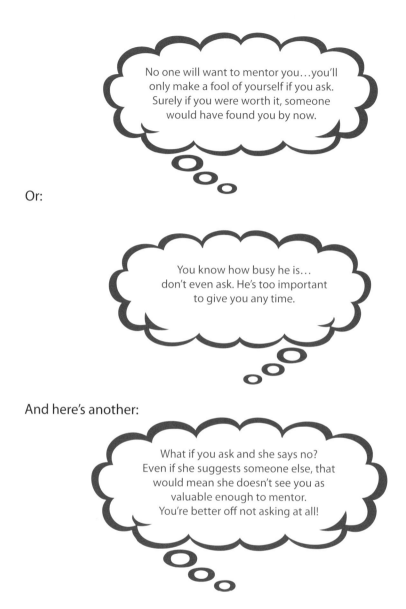

Or:

And here's another:

If the voice inside your head is telling you any of these stories, ignore it! With a planned approach, a little structure, and your willingness to take responsibility for making it work, you can approach any potential mentor and stand a great chance of getting a "yes" to your request!

The worksheets will help you structure your approach and your time so you can establish solid mentoring relationships. When you've identified potential mentors, use the worksheets to develop your plan and your approach.

Career Ownership

Mentoring: Finding & Respecting Your Mentors

Ways to ensure a "win-win" mentoring relationship

The most valuable mentoring relationships have goals, a structure and clear expectations and boundaries. Both the Mentor and the Mentee understand that excellent interpersonal skills foster powerful learning. Use this worksheet to shape a mentoring relationship that works for both you and the Mentor.

The best mentoring relationships have:

1. Goals

2. Structure & Expectations

3. Follow-up & Follow-through

4. Skills awareness

Goals: Consider and write before you approach a Mentor

- What do you want to learn?

- Why are you approaching this person? What do you think you can learn from that person better than from any other?

- Complete the Mentoring Competencies Assessment Worksheet for ideas on possible learning areas.

Structure: Do your planning before you approach a Mentor

- Consider logistics and organize your thoughts

  - Logistics

  1. Consider when, where, why, how: Define what you want to learn and visualize how the mentoring relationship might work.

  2. Consider length of relationship: what kind of commitment are you asking of the Mentor? Is it reasonable given what you know about the Mentor? Is it reasonable for the goals you have? A meeting on occasion? Meetings two times a month for four months? This is negotiable, but you must put thought into your request.

  3. Consider meeting options: Will meeting over a cup of coffee work? Or maybe a quarterly breakfast meeting? How about a telephone call every two weeks? Check-in by email?

 Career Ownership

Mentoring: Finding & Respecting Your Mentors

4. Define the responsibilities you're willing to take on in a Mentee role. Consider being responsible for scheduling, sending an agenda ahead of time, and completing an email with your learning commitments that will follow each meeting.

5. Be clear on what you're seeking from the Mentor: I'd like you to show me how to improve my presentation skills. Or, I'd like you to give me feedback on how I can work effectively within my team.

- Consider the Mentor and how you show respect

  1. Contacting, boundaries: be respectful of time and approach; ask about preferences and "best times" to connect.

  2. Preparation, agenda: plan to set an agenda and send it prior to each meeting so the Mentor can prepare; be ready to work your way through the agenda unless the Mentor takes the lead.

  3. Ask the Mentor: What would make it easy for you to mentor me?

  4. Be sensitive to differences: respect busy schedules; generational values; experience levels.

  5. The Mentor needs to know that you are serious about learning.

Follow-up and follow-through is important

- Take responsibility for both follow-up and follow-through

  1. Send a follow-up email to your Mentor after the meeting making note of your learning commitments and thanking him or her for meeting.

  2. Be prepared during your next meeting to review your learning and share your observations around it.

  3. Your Mentor will know you are serious about learning when you show up prepared—not as an empty vessel to be filled!

Career Ownership
Mentoring: Finding & Respecting Your Mentors

<u>Consider the skills below as minimal for a sound relationship</u>

- •Active listening

- •Possibility and innovative thinking

- •Ask questions from curiosity (non-judgmental)

- •Developing trusting environment

- •Giving feedback and Feeding forward

If you're unclear about any of these skills, ask your Mentor to suggest how you can improve them and how you can focus on them while you are meeting.

The template below can be used to help you structure a beneficial mentoring relationship for both the Mentor and the Mentee!

Mentor: _____ ; **Set-up:** _____

(e.g. one hour meeting over lunch each quarter)

   1. What do you want to learn? List 6-8 items

   _____

   _____

   _____

   _____

   2. Select 2 or 3 items from above. Create questions and an informal agenda to structure your learning discussion with the Mentor.

   _____

   _____

   _____

   _____

   3. Before you finish, ask: What specific actions or suggestions do you have that would continue my learning in this area?

   4. If you're willing to take accountability, tell your Mentor: As a follow-up, I will contact you via (method) within (time frame) and give you a status report of my learning and progress.

Career Ownership

Potential Development Areas: General Competencies

Review the knowledge, skills and attitudes below and rate each based upon your need and desire to develop in that particular area. Use this as a guide for talking with your mentor about skills development.

Skill	Low Need				High Need
Stress management	1	2	3	4	5
Written communication skills	1	2	3	4	5
Planning & organization skills	1	2	3	4	5
Negotiations skills	1	2	3	4	5
Written communications skills	1	2	3	4	5
Problem-solving skills	1	2	3	4	5
Resilience skills	1	2	3	4	5
Trust-building skills	1	2	3	4	5
Active listening skills	1	2	3	4	5
'Questioning from curiosity' skill	1	2	3	4	5
Emotional self-awareness	1	2	3	4	5
Empathy	1	2	3	4	5
Professionalism/Understanding perceptions	1	2	3	4	5
Balancing work and personal demands	1	2	3	4	5
Influence skills	1	2	3	4	5
Change-ability/agility	1	2	3	4	5
Lifelong learning attitude	1	2	3	4	5
Communication Styles	1	2	3	4	5
Teamwork skills	1	2	3	4	5
Conflict management	1	2	3	4	5
Service orientation	1	2	3	4	5
Organization awareness (culture & politics)	1	2	3	4	5
Presentation skills	1	2	3	4	5
Feedback & feed-forward skills	1	2	3	4	5

> *Every sale has five basic obstacles: no need, no money, no hurry, no desire, no trust.*
>
> - Zig Ziglar,
> Legendary Motivational Speaker

Chapter 10: Use Keycard for Entry: Craft Your Business Case

Once you determine how you best align with your organization and define development and career paths, you must make a business case because you are, after all, requesting a business decision. If you cannot present a sound business case, a sale as Zig Ziglar references, then it makes no sense for the organization to approve your proposal.

Ziglar's quote (above) is a good model for assembling a business case. Speak to each potential obstacle in your proposal: need, money, time, desire and trust. Use these items as an outline to help you frame your proposal.

The worksheet included here provides guidance for you to develop a business case or proposal that includes these items. Your case will be structured, then, to:

- prove the need for your proposal and its alignment with strategy;

- show economic benefit (new revenue, avoided cost, etc.);

- define an advantageous time frame (within strategic plan);

- outline the benefits and specific value to the organization; and

- demonstrate your trustworthiness.

As you have worked at defining best career actions, you will have made connections and learned about business direction that will make your case. Your mentors can lend their critical thinking to your rationale and conclusions. Everything you put into your case must work toward aligning your direction with the organization's.

Why you need a business case

1. You are redefining your role in an organization as that of "career owner" rather than an employee "waiting to be picked." Any role change requires a different set of behaviors, whether it's a move to "home" or "pet" or "career" ownership. In a business setting, your responsibility includes making a case for your partner's (the organization) consideration. You've collected the facts to support your proposal and a business case helps you lay out your thinking in a logical fashion. Most successful business people try to make fact-based decisions, and limit emotional ones.

2. Developing a business case or proposal helps clarify your thinking, identify holes, and collect everything you need to make a solid case. This includes advocates and broad-based "buy-in."

3. A business proposal helps you focus on "wiifm" (what's in it for me), or better yet, "what's in it for both of us." Most businesses recognize that a "win-win" for both the organization and employees creates greater satisfaction that transfers to customers. But often an organization doesn't know how to create a win-win: its structures and outdated practices from a more rigid time trump common sense. Your proposal provides a model and a method to achieve the elusive alignment that organizations need now but struggle to achieve.

Pitfalls to avoid

- **Expecting that your case will be approved because you see it as perfect.** Can you recall a time when you interviewed for a position or a promotion for which you knew you were the absolute best candidate and were crushed when you didn't get the offer? Constructing your case and expecting that the decision-makers will see it the same way is naïve at best and presumptuous at worst.

Maybe you have put together the perfect case, but it's always wise to allow for surprises. Consider these possibilities:

- there's been a change in the market since you put your case together
- your biggest advocate has left the organization and you're experiencing fallout
- unplanned budget cuts put a hold on all workforce changes
- one of the decision-makers is new to the organization and wants to learn the company better before she agrees with your case
- you missed some competitive intelligence that makes your proposal untimely or iffy
- you didn't count on reorganization plans that will send your case back to the drawing board

Does this mean that you give up? No, it simply means that you consider a "Plan B" when you construct your proposal and be willing to take another run at it with a better level of knowledge, more support, or revisions that will strengthen your case.

- **Ignoring or underestimating the politics of your organization.** Like it or not, most organizations live and breathe some level of political activity and you must manage this as you craft your business case. You might do that through mentors or other relationships, but also give real thought to sharpening your own interpersonal and social skills: these are the backbone of organizational politics (good and not-so-good).

Recognize, too, that relationship skills are also the backbone of collaboration, innovation and excellent service; it would be a mistake for you to dismiss them because 'you're good at your job.' Improving your relationship-building and maintenance skills is a politically wise move and a necessity for any work in any organization.

Career Ownership

Crafting the Business Case / Proposal

In crafting your proposal for your career direction or next career step, there are many business case and proposal templates available. You can search the web or any number of business books to find one you like, or your organization may have a preferred format for formal proposals. If you're not curtailed by a required form, keep your final product brief—between two and four pages.

Whatever format you choose, the cardinal rule of preparation is "WIIFM, or what's in it for me?" – meaning your audience! Keeping your audience in mind as you craft your proposal will guide you to include pertinent and persuasive reasoning for everyone who is involved in the decision process.

Taking each of the five obstacles described, you can use the following table to consider information and tailor your message to each person in your audience. Use names of the appropriate decision makers for your own proposal.

Decision Makers / Obstacles	VP / Department	Human Resources	Manager
(need) What's the need?			
(need) How is the need aligned with business strategy?			
(money) What are economic benefits to the organization?			

Career Ownership

Crafting the Business Case / Proposal

Decision Makers Obstacles	VP / Department	Human Resources	Manager
(hurry) **What timeframe supports the strategic plan?**			
(desire) **What are benefits, the value to the organization? (include your value here, too)**			
(trust) **How can you support your claims to reduce risk?**			
(other)			

Determine the most important obstacle(s) to each audience member and speak to those barriers in your written proposal and during any presentation. As you complete the boxes in the table, you'll easily see where you have holes, either in your data or your reasoning. Get your mentors' support during this preparation; their perspectives may identify things you haven't considered.

Use a simple, straight-forward presentation format that includes:

1. Your Proposal Recommendation

2. Background in support of the recommendation

3. Rationale for the recommendation; response to anticipated objections

4. Timetable for suggested action

5. Financial impact including time and other resources

6. The Ask, your specific request of the listener(s)

Career Ownership

Crafting the Business Case / Proposal

Your proposal can be as simple as the example following: a direct, factual, easy-to-read communication. Or, depending upon your audience and the cultural of your organization, you may want to prepare a power point presentation complete with graphics, charts and data. Knowing your audience and what appeals to each of them is your best guide. Again, you can check with your mentors and manager (if appropriate) for their insight.

Proposal: A Growth Strategy
For XYZ Enterprise Area

Prepared by:
Date:

Recommendation

Background

Explanation/Rationale

Resources Impact

Timing

The Ask

> *Find something you love to do and you'll never have to work a day in your life*
>
> - Harvey MacKay,
> Author and Inspirational Business Speaker

Conclusion: Career Ownership: it's a wrap

I really hope that you've enjoyed this read, but more than that I hope you've been spurred, energized, and inspired. We're living in a time of great change and the choice is yours: you can let that change happen to you or you can make it work for you. Career Ownership helps you set a confident direction if you choose to make those changes work for you.

A few final thoughts for you to consider, in case you haven't already:

1. Recognize that career ownership may work in your current organization or it may not. "Time to move" may mean "inside" or "out"—only you can say.

2. Recognize that career ownership isn't for everyone, just like home ownership isn't for everyone. Chances are very good that jobs aren't going away anytime soon, so there will still be plenty around. If it's really a "job" you want, acknowledge it. And at the same time, recognize that you might spend more time searching for your next job—and your next —than you would like.

3. Recognize that career ownership isn't for every organization. Sometimes a change in "how we've always done things" takes time; sometimes the organization just doesn't see the need.

That's no reason for you to wait. You can take ownership of your career and tell someone else about it. You can create a group of Career Owners within—or outside of—your organization. Your manager or group leader may see the benefits to your area or your department and encourage everyone toward career ownership. You can move forward—taking ownership of your career—if you choose it.

The Question:

Does the misery of doing work that doesn't fit, doesn't challenge, and doesn't interest you or the fear of being downsized outweigh the fear of taking responsibility for your career?

Words of wisdom:

1. Career ownership is an unknown direction for many workers; use a guide—a Career Ownership Coach—who can help you map the 'unknown' so you get to your destination.

2. Living in a 'seam' is challenging: we're tasked with moving from one place to another without clear direction. Since 'work' is what funds our lives, 'jumping the seam' is critical. Career ownership, again, provides a map.

3. You'll never do anything better than when you're doing work you love. I know…because I do.

Appendix #1: Career Ownership Worksheets

Web link: http://WorkforceChange.com/CareerOwnership

Foundation & Fit

1. Who I Am
2. What I Value
3. What Energizes Me
4. What My Talents Are
5. Where My Skills Lie
6. How I Work Best
7. What Possibilities Fit Me
8. Identifying Targets
9. THREADS: Finding My Life Themes

Leveraging your Strengths

1. My Talents and How I Use Them
2. Themes and Success
3. How Others See Your Talents

Learning about the Organization

1. What's the Big Picture?
2. Considering Growth Areas: Smaller Picture

Finding Mentors & Matches

1. Finding & Respecting Your Mentors
2. Mentoring Competencies Assessment

Making the Business Case

1. Crafting Your Business Case / Proposal

Appendix # 2: References and Resources

Books

Buckingham, Marcus. Go Put Your Strengths to Work. New York: Simon & Schuster, 2007.

Buckingham, Marcus & Donald O. Clifton, Ph.D. Now, Discover Your Strengths. New York: Simon & Schuster, 2001.

Dweck, Carol S. Ph.D. Mindset: The New Psychology of Success. New York: Ballantine Books, 2008 trade paperback edition.

Godin, Seth. Linchpin: Are You Indispensable? New York: Penguin Group, 2010.

Jamison, Kaleel. The Nibble Theory and the Kernel of Power. New Jersey: Paulist Press, 1984.

Pink, Daniel. A Whole New Mind: Why Right Brainers Will Rule the Future. New York: Penguin Group, 2005, 2006.

Pink, Daniel. Drive: The Surprising Truth About What Motivates Us. New York: Penguin Group, 2009.

Rath, Tom. Strengthsfinder 2.0. New York: Gallup Press, 2007.

Online Resources

Gallup Inc., Gallup Consulting. "Gallup Economic Weekly Averages," Underemployment and Job Creation Indices updated weekly. Web: http://www.gallup.com/consulting/ Gallup-Consulting

Gallup Inc., Strengthsfinder 2.0 Assessment. Information on research, forums and purchase. Web: http://www. strengthsfinder.com

About the Author

Janine Moon, a Master Certified Career Coach, has spent thirty plus years mentoring, growing, developing and coaching people—both individually and within organization development initiatives.

She has experienced "work" from many perspectives: from the handle of a hoe on her family's northwest Ohio farm to the vice president's desk at a utility company. This "Corporate Wars" veteran has also directed enterprise and not-for-profit organizations, developed and implemented human capital strategies, and coached hundreds of individuals to define their authentic work direction and trust themselves to pursue it.

Janine has taught in secondary and college institutions; trained line workers, professionals and executives; delivered conference keynotes and moderated break-outs; facilitated large and small groups, both agreeable and antagonistic; designed and led change initiatives; and coached professionals, teams and C-level leaders. Clients range from individuals to a diverse blend of corporations and organizations: media and technology, insurance, utilities, manufacturing, governments, professional services firms, and education and non-profits.

Janine's work, Career Ownership, is original and unique in its approach to career development inside organizations. The program is based on Janine's considerable leadership within organizations, her knowledge of economies and productivity, 21st century global competition, and her deep understanding and extensive experience with what engages individuals to do their best work and connect deeply with an organization's mission.

Janine provides keynotes, seminars and tailored programs on Career Ownership, 21st Century Leadership and "The Hard Truth About the Soft Stuff"… the truth that engaged and committed employees out-think and out-do the competition every time! As a sought-after speaker, Janine's delivery is highly interactive, thought-provoking and challenging to "we've-always-done-it-this-way" thinking. Her engaging style motivates listeners to sync their outdated world views with the reality of today's global business environment.

Janine holds a Master's degree from The Ohio State University and a Bachelor's of Science from Bowling Green State University. She has achieved certification as a Master Certified Career Coach (one of five in the country) from The Career Coach Institute where she serves as an Instructor and Mentor Coach. She is a Professional Member of the National Speakers Association (NSA), the 2008 President of the Ohio Chapter and a member of the International Coaching Federation. Janine also serves as advisor to Franklin University's MBA Executive Coaching Program and as an MBA Adjunct Faculty member.

Order Form

Fax orders: 614.488-1458. Send this form.

Telephone orders: 614.488-6876.

Email orders: Janine@WorkforceChange.com

Web site orders: http://WorkforceChange.com/CareerOwnership

Postal orders— send this form to:

CompassPoint Coaching LLC
2015 Arlington Avenue
Columbus, Ohio 43212

Book Order Mailing instructions:

Send to _____

Street address _____

City, State, Zip _____

Telephone contact #: _____

Book Order	
Quantity	*Amount*
_____ **Career Ownership: Creating 'Job Security' in Any Economy** ($24.95)	_____
Sales tax of $1.68 per book for Ohio residents	_____
Shipping and handling ($4.00 for first book; $1.50 for each additional book)	_____
Total amount enclosed	_____

Quantity discounts available. Please allow 2 weeks for shipping.

Method of payment

❑ Check or money order enclosed (made payable to CompassPoint Coaching LLC)

❑ Master Card   ❑ Visa

Card Number: _____ Expiration date: _____

Name on card: _____ Address _____

Signature _____

❑ **Please contact me about Janine's Career Ownership speaking, seminars or consulting**

Order Form

Fax orders: 614.488-1458. Send this form.

Telephone orders: 614.488-6876.

Email orders: Janine@WorkforceChange.com

Web site orders: http://WorkforceChange.com/CareerOwnership

Postal orders— send this form to:

CompassPoint Coaching LLC
2015 Arlington Avenue
Columbus, Ohio 43212

Book Order Mailing instructions:

Send to _____

Street address _____

City, State, Zip _____

Telephone contact #: _____

Book Order

Quantity		Amount
_____	**Career Ownership: Creating 'Job Security' in Any Economy** ($24.95)	_____
	Sales tax of $1.68 per book for Ohio residents	_____
	Shipping and handling ($4.00 for first book; $1.50 for each additional book)	_____
	Total amount enclosed	_____

Quantity discounts available. Please allow 2 weeks for shipping.

Method of payment

❑ Check or money order enclosed (made payable to CompassPoint Coaching LLC)

❑ Master Card   ❑ Visa

Card Number: _____ Expiration date: _____

Name on card: _____ Address _____

Signature _____

❑ **Please contact me about Janine's Career Ownership speaking, seminars or consulting**